ALMOST STRAIGHT DOWN

THE MIDDLE

ALMOST STRAIGHT DOWN THE MIDDLE

A GOLFER'S COLLECTION

CHRIS PLUMRIDGE

Queen Anne Press

C2160094 99

First published in 1993 by
Queen Anne Press
a division of Lennard Associates Ltd
Mackerye End
Harpenden
Herts AL5 5DR

796·352

CE

ISBN 1 85291 531 5

British Library Cataloguing in Publication Data
is available

Jacket design by Cooper Wilson
Jacket illustration by John Beswick

Printed and bound in Great Britain by
Butler & Tanner Ltd, Frome and London

ACKNOWLEDGEMENT

The author would like to thank the Editors and Sports Editors of the
following publications for their good taste and judgement in publishing
the pieces featured in this collection in the first place:
*Sunday Telegraph, The Times, Independent, Guardian, Golf Illustrated,
Golf International, Golf Magazine* and *Punch.*

CONTENTS

For
Vanessa, Joanna and Jessica

IN THE BEGINNING

AN INTRODUCTION

Long ago, just after the era of the firmament and the crawlies, primitive man and woman grew accustomed to taking long walks in the countryside. Their motivation for this exercise was quite simply the necessity to eat, for tracking down the odd woolly mammoth meant long days away from the comfort of the cave.

As a means of passing the time on these trips to the prehistoric supermarket, primitive man and woman would arm themselves with sticks from a nearby hickory tree and take casual swipes at loose stones in their path. Occasionally, when the mood took them, they would place the stone on a dried-up piece of pterodactyl dropping and give the stone a real clout. Gradually they realised that the stone went further if the hickory stick was fashioned with a bulbous lump on the end and so, dearly beloved, that is how they spent their walking hours.

Now one day, our primitive couple came across a particularly attractive piece of real estate. The land rose and fell in gentle undulations, flowering shrubs grew in abundance, each attended by a brightly coloured humming-bird, butterflies and bees flitted to and fro, the grass was a verdant green and in the distance a group of pine trees shimmered on the horizon. "Hey, Eve," said the man, "this looks a great place for some stone-hitting. See that tree down there, why don't we both hit our stones towards it and the one who reaches the tree in the fewest hits gets out of the fig-leaf washing tonight? I'll start from here and you start a little nearer."

So off they went towards the tree, laughing happily on their way, and they both reached the tree in five hits apiece. It was then they noticed the tree. It was quite unlike any other tree in the vicinity. Its leaves were a pale golden colour, its bark was as smooth as Ben Crenshaw's putting-stroke and it emitted a faint perfume while, as it stood there bathed in sunshine, the beams glanced off a perfectly rounded, large, tempting golden apple. "I'll bet our EC subsidy that ain't no French Golden Delicious," muttered the woman. "Leave it be,

Eve!" shouted the man. "What with crop-spraying, pesticides and CFCs, you can't be too careful these days, although I must say that's a juicy looking apple."

As they stood there admiring the apple, there was a rustle in the foliage of the tree. A long green snake slithered through the leaves and fixed the couple with a beady stare. The couple recoiled in fear. "Don't be afraid," hissed the snake, "us serpents aren't all bad. Look, I'm in the promotions business myself and what I have to tell you can only be to your advantage. I was watching you earlier and I said to myself, Sidney, that's my name you see, but you can call me Sid – Sid, I said, you don't see stone-hitters like that more than once in an aeon. Potential, and I mean potential, is unlimited and I mean unlimited. Then I said to myself, c'mon Sid, leave it out, these people probably don't want to become better stone-hitters, they're probably quite happy hitting the stone the way they do, why bother them?"

"We wouldn't mind hitting the stone just a little better," said the couple, somewhat nervously.

"Aah," continued the snake, "can I spot them or can I spot them? Look, I don't want to press you unduly, but there was another couple through here yesterday who are coming back tomorrow and they are very interested in my deal, and I mean very interested. But as it's you and you're here, well, need I say more?"

"What's the deal?" chorused the couple excitedly.

The snake coiled itself a little more tightly round the branch. "The deal is this," said the snake, its eyes glittering, "you want to hit the stone better, you want to hit it further, maybe you want to move the stone in different directions through the air. Maybe, one day, and forgive me for being immodest, you will want a couple of little stone-hitters to carry on after you. Perhaps you might want to form your own stone-hitters' club where you can exchange stories with your friends. All these things and more can be yours if you just take a bite out of the apple on this tree."

The couple looked at one another apprehensively. They looked at the snake, which nodded its head towards the apple. The man reached up and plucked the apple from the tree. He examined it, took a bite and passed it across to the woman, who also took a bite. The apple was deliciously succulent, crisp and sweet. They devoured it hungrily and, pausing only to thank the snake, who was looking at them with a sly grin on its face, they picked up their sticks and walked back up the slope.

The sun was still shining, the land still looked as appealing, the shrubs were still blooming and the bees, butterflies and humming-birds were still busy. The man put down his stone, eager to try out the new powers the apple had given him. He hit the stone. It flew off viciously to the right and plummeted down into the depths of a flowering shrub. The man said a new word which he hadn't used before. The woman then put down her stone and hit it. It too flew off to the right into a shrub. She also used a new word. They found their stones and hacked them out of the bushes, but with their next hits, the stones were back in the bushes or behind a tree or in a stream.

They laboured on through the day. Sometimes the stone would fly straight and true but more often than not it would fly off at a tangent. As the day drew to a close they decided that their only recourse was to return to the tree and ask the snake why their stone-hitting, instead of improving, had steadily worsened. When they reached the tree it had changed. Its leaves were an ordinary green colour, its bark was rough and gnarled and its branches stuck out at odd angles similar to Eamonn Darcy's backswing. The snake was nowhere to be seen but pinned to the tree was a note: "How do you like them apples?" it read.

And that, my children, is how sin first came into the world. Fortunately, we are all still having a whale of a time.

(1984)

At the Club

Women on Top

Since we are presently in a Leap Year and February 29th is not far away, it seems an appropriate time to touch on the role of women in golf.

The poet Shelley thought he had hit the nail on the head when he stated: "Can man be free if woman be a slave?" but in truth he was totally incorrect. It is us poor males who are the victims of the world's longest-running con-trick with regard to our relationship with the opposite sex.

Nature plays its first cruel trick on us by allowing us to enter this world in the presence of a woman. There we are, naked and helpless, and before we have hardly had time to draw breath, we are clamped on the nipple.

This is done, of course, to achieve woman's first objective, that is to keep us quiet so that she can get on with nattering to her neighbour in the next bed. I ask you, in all seriousness, what man could retain any shred of dignity in such a situation?

Having established her immediate superiority over us at an early age, woman is quite content to let us develop along the misguided lines that it is us who are superior simply because of our greater physical strength. Just when we think that rucking in the loose maul and sharing the communal bath afterwards is the closest a chap is likely to get to heaven, then old Mother Nature (she's a woman too) whips in a fierce left hook by enabling us to notice, yes, you've guessed it – girls!

The sight of these strange winsome creatures whose physiques contain many interesting bumps and curves hits us like an express train.

Forgetting that these new objects of our attentions are merely junior versions of the mothers who exposed us so ridiculously in our earlier years, we plough after them in a lemming-like charge. Too late we realise that it is not us who are doing the chasing, it is the girls who are setting the pace, leading us unsuspectingly into a series of carefully laid traps. Suddenly we are caught, enmeshed in the allure of a pretty face, and there is no escape.

An example of this occurred many years ago when a group of us males used to gather at the club and play regularly. Those were halcyon days – 72 holes each weekend, endless games of poker in the bar afterwards, then off to the local rugby club dance to chat up the local talent.

One day, one of our number arrived on the 1st tee wearing a lime green sweater into which had been woven a pattern of pink teddy bears holding hands in an endless chain of cuddly awfulness. "What is that?" we exclaimed in unison. "You mean the sweater," he replied, a wistful expression crossing his features. "Oh, Jenny knitted it for me."

We knew at once he was doomed and, sure enough, the tumbril came to take him to his wedding a few months later and we never saw him again.

In the face of such onslaughts, it is hardly surprising that men have taken refuge in whatever sanctuary they can find.

In bygone days, golf provided the perfect haven for when the game first took root on the barren approaches of the Scottish coastline the prevailing conditions – rain, wind, sleet, snow, freezing fog – meant that golf courses were no place for the gentler sex.

Having persuaded their womenfolk that the game could render their complexions the texture of a brogue shoe, the men set about building a citadel of masculinity that would repel all attacks.

Clubhouses were built on austere lines with nary a curve or a soft line on them. Entrance doors were constructed from seasoned oak so that only the heaviest Amazon could force them open, floors were uncarpeted and furniture was solid and uncomfortable.

Of course, it couldn't last. The women became suspicious of their menfolk's driving urge to be off to the links. Surely, they thought, such a consuming passion couldn't be provided by a mere game. There must be other, more sinister, reasons for these prolonged absences from the nest. So the women investigated, infiltrated and finally breached the defences. We have been in retreat ever since.

A few clubs are still fighting a rearguard action but it is a futile one. The die is cast and it is only a matter of time before the last bastion falls beneath the tramp of this monstrous regiment.

What, if anything, can we poor males do to protect ourselves? Very little I'm afraid. There is nothing for it but to lie back and think of St Andrews. (1984)

A MOVING EXPERIENCE

"Oi, mush," bellowed the Editor as he left another weal across my back with his sjambok, "your reader has been wanting to know why your ugly features have been so infrequently exposed recently at the top of this page. Unfortunately we cannot tell him that you've been run over by a bus so it looks like you've got some explaining to do."

Well, dear reader, may I first commend you for your loyalty and hope that the following explanation will appease you. The truth is I've been moving – in fact by the time you read this I shall have moved and the nightmare will be over. It's a nightmare which began over two years ago when I realised that Parkinson's law, or a variation of it, could easily be applied to my working conditions.

Using the spare bedroom as an office has many disadvantages, not least being the occasional guest dossing down among the books and magazines which are an integral part of the golf writer's life. Thus as the work expanded to fill more than the space allotted the decision to up sticks and resettle was made.

In such a situation, the ideal equation is to find a suitable new abode for the minimum price while at the same time you have a queue of people all waving blank cheques as they clamour to purchase your property. It doesn't, however, work that way.

After much hunting through the local newspaper and among the estate agents we quickly learned that des. family res. with much charm and old world character meant that anybody standing over four feet in height had to walk around with a permanent stoop to avoid bumping into the old world character. Or "easy access to the motorway" meant that the hard shoulder was just at the bottom of the garden. Eventually we found a suitable dwelling for which our offer was accepted and now it only remained for us to sell our house.

Looking round other people's houses seems to have a strange effect on the viewers. They tend to fall into certain categories. First, there are the professional house-viewers. These are people who have absolutely no intention of buying your house, or indeed anybody else's, but are obsessed with seeing how other people live. They usually make an appointment to view on Sunday afternoon around tea-time and pitch up on the doorstep with sundry relatives in tow so that as you show them round you feel like a guide with a party of American tourists. The professional house-viewer invariably exclaims "How lovely" or "This is nice" as you move from room to room, but this is merely a softening up process to persuade you to get cracking with the tea and crumpets. If this is not forthcoming then the professional house-viewer can turn nasty and leave in a huff.

This type of viewer is infinitely preferable to the Attila the Hun viewer. Attila and his hordes arrive on your doorstep and begin a metaphorical rape and pillage of your house. Attila believes that as your house is for sale then you don't actually own it any more, and as you show him round your house he and his family systematically destroy your mode of living. "Of course," says Attila, "we'll have to paint the whole house." Or: "You'll be leaving all the curtains and carpets in for the price, won't you?" By the time Attila has finished finding fault with your home you wonder whatever induced you to live there in the first place.

After two years of showing people round our house, we now have a fair idea of who is a serious buyer and who isn't, but selling your own house is only fifty per cent of the nightmare. From being a seller extolling the virtues of your own house, you then have to cross the lines and become a hard-nosed purchaser hot on the trail of a bargain.

Having been unable to sell our house quickly enough we lost the purchase of the first house we wanted to buy. Then we sold our house again but could not find a suitable house to buy and again we lost the sale of our house. Then we finally found what we were looking for. Ideally situated, the house had plenty of room and a large garden. There was only one major drawback. The owner of the house was a little old lady who had lived there for the past forty years, the last twenty of which she had been on her own and consequently things had run down a little. It wasn't that the house was derelict, but it certainly wasn't straight out of *Homes & Gardens*. In order to look round the garden one needed a machete and a gang of bearers and as we waded through the undergrowth I felt certain I glimpsed a Japanese soldier flitting through the trees.

Here's a warning to all would-be house purchasers. Avoid little old ladies who have lived in the same house for forty years for they move, if they move at all, in a mysterious way.

Now, fourteen months later, the whole business has been drawn to a conclusion. The little old lady has finally departed, we have sold our house and the builders are in. Life will hopefully now take on a more measured pace free from the frantic tidying up that occurs when people provide half an hour's notice before coming to view your house and free also from the mad dash across the countryside to view a house that is on offer £10,000 more than you can afford but you hope you can knock the price down a little.

What, you may ask, has all this to do with golf? Very little really, except that instead of being ten minutes away from my golf club I am now only two. Perhaps it was all worth it after all.
(1983)

THE GENERAL RULES OF GOLF

I expect you have been wondering about the Meaning of Life. You know the sort of thing – why are we here, where are we going and is it possible to hit a 1-iron from a cuppy lie through a left to right cross-wind? Burning questions as to whether there is life after the lateral hip shift need to be answered if we are to find Peace and Eternal Happiness.

As a disciple of the Temple of the Ever Hopeful, I have spent many contemplative hours fasting on the top of a mountain (actually, it was the pulpit tee of the short 7th hole at my club, but that's because Wednesday's child has vertigo), and my musings revealed the following General Rules of Golf.

The first tee shot following a lesson travels 20 yards along the ground.
The shortest distance between the ball and the target is never a straight line.
Electric trolleys break down at the furthest point from the clubhouse.
The pencil needed to mark a card is always at the bottom of the bag.
And when it is found, it is broken.
Immediately waterproofs are donned it stops raining.
Waterproof trousers cannot be removed without falling over.
When there is one minute left to get to the 1st tee, a shoelace breaks.
The ball nestling in a footprint in a bunker is always yours.
The only available space in the club car park is furthest from the locker room.
Rare mid-week rounds of golf take place in the midst of a visiting society.
Greens are hollow-tined and dressed the day before a competition.
The newer the golf ball, the greater its propensity for disappearing.
If the club is burgled, your clubs are never stolen.
And if they are, you are under-insured.
The reserve golf glove kept for wet weather has shrunk.
The number of practice balls recovered is always fewer than the number hit.

If you find your ball in the woods, it is unplayable.

If a professional finds his ball in the woods, not only is it playable but he can hit it on the green.

The one remaining set of new clubs in the professional's shop was made especially for you.

In a pro-am, you are the last to drive off after your professional and partners have all hit screamers.

When you drive your car to a pro-am, you are caught in an impenetrable traffic jam.

The latest piece of written instruction never works on the course.

The "yips" is something which afflicts other people. Until now.

The sand in the bunkers is never the right texture for your particular method.

Television commentators invariably tell you what you can already see.

Someone always says "One" when your ball falls off the tee peg.

The same person always says "Never up, never in" when you leave a putt of three feet short.

The same person always says "Why didn't you do that the first time?" when you hit a rasping stroke with a provisional ball.

The same person has to be led away before you fell him with your sand-wedge.

There is no truth in the theory that if you know how to shank you will never do so.

Passing lorry-drivers always shout "Fore" at the top of your backswing.

The best drive of the day finishes in a divot mark.

Delicate chips over bunkers always catch the top of the bank and fall back.

Out-of-bounds fences are located a foot the wrong side of your ball.

A hole-in-one is achieved when playing alone.

Whenever you take your clubs on a golfing holiday, you leave your game behind.

During the first round with a brand new set of clubs, the ball has to be played from a road.

Golf balls that are supposed not to cut have never been "thinned" out of a bunker.

Shots that finish close to the pin are never as close when you get there.

It's always the next round that will find you playing your normal game.

The General Rules of Golf affect only you.

(1986)

DRESSING TO KILL

While the standard of dress among male golfers has risen in recent years, there are some areas where it still leaves something to be desired.

Jeans, T-shirts and sneakers are all too prevalent, particularly among the young, and at the risk of being branded a reactionary I was delighted to see that this year's Tillman Trophy will have a code of dress for both on and off the course at Royal St George's in June.

The first edict is that jeans and training shoes are forbidden, and hurrah for that! Jackets and ties or polo-neck sweaters must be worn in the dining room, reading room and members' bar. And, finally, neat trousers, shirts and sweaters are expected on the course.

Since most of the competitors will be under 25, then these rules should eliminate any "rock generation" attire. On the other hand, I know a good few golfers who will shortly be collecting their bus passes whose interpretation of that dress code might be correct, but whose execution is lamentable.

The way we dress for golf reflects our personality and our ability at the game. There are still those players who believe that golf is some kind of rustic pursuit and appear in gardeners' cast-offs; others try to follow fashion but invariably get it wrong. As a rule, though, dressing for golf is like the handicap system and divides players into four categories.

CATEGORY 1: This is the quiet man who wears white shoes, dark slacks, white sports shirt and light blue sweater with the sleeves rolled up to reveal tanned forearms.

Light brown golf gloves, just out of the wrapper, show that he does not fool around on the course, as does the tan. He rarely fails to break par whenever he plays and, if he could spare the time, would play the big amateur events. Can be recognised by the roughness of his right hand when shaking hands.

Has a steely glint in icy-blue eyes and, when he picks up a club, looks as though he was born with it. Doesn't talk much on the course except to say: "That puts me three up, I think."

CATEGORY 2: Found at clubs with brown leather armchairs and members to match. Heavily dubbined brown brogue shoes, dark green socks and quiet check plus-fours with dark grey sweater and a small concession to modernity in the shape of a buttoned sports shirt in navy-blue.

Check cap hides distinguished grey hair and his conversation embraces price-earnings ratios, the disaster of the incumbent government's economic policies and how overcrowded the course is, due to the fact there are six other players on the course, none of whom are within two holes of him.

Plays his golf with three other gentlemen of similar disposition and rarely enters competitions in case he is partnered with someone of lower social rank.

CATEGORY 3: This player has fallen heavily under the influence of professional golf. His golf shirt is festooned with logos and he has a large gold medallion hanging outside the shirt.

Calls everyone "John", no matter what their name is, and says things like: "Great ball, John!" Believes that if he dresses like the pros he will play like them. But his main objective on the course is to do the ball as violent an injury as possible.

CATEGORY 4: Known as "the Slob", he arrives at the club in a 15-year-old car and doesn't bother to change in the locker room. Crumpled grey trousers with plastic belt are set off by a mole-coloured sweater ravaged by moths and an off-white shirt with an obscure regimental tie.

He is probably running to fat, hence the plastic belt to maintain the trouser-level above his stomach. Inclined to perspire and, when he has finished playing, the Slob wafts into the bar on a cloud of rich, unpleasant odour, believing that real men should smell like real men.

Has an indescribable slice which his opponents regard as the only thing in his favour as it keeps him away from them on the course.

Referring back to the dress codes of the clubhouse, an amusing little exchange occurred at a club near London where the Cambridge University Golf team were due to play a match.

Four senior members of the club were in the clubhouse, just prior to going out to play after lunch, when the Cambridge team came in. They looked perfectly presentable except for one of their number who was dressed in trousers and an open-necked shirt. "Excuse me," said one of the members. "I hope you are not going into the bar dressed like that."

"As a matter of fact, I am."

"You most certainly are not," stuttered the irate member. "Jackets and ties are the rule at this club."

"Perhaps it has escaped your notice," replied the Cambridge student, "that I am a girl."
(1991)

The Wait-listed Game

Golfers everywhere have good reason to lament the Lamont Budget. It's going to cost us more to drive to the club at weekends, more to have a drink and smoke in the bar after a round, and the purchase of that gleaming new set of irons may have to wait.

We shall all have to learn to be straighter, as the loss of a new ball may bring further economic hardship; subscriptions will also rise due to the new VAT rate.

Whether this will signal mass resignations from golf clubs is doubtful, for membership of a club is likely to remain a golfer's most cherished possession. For those people aspiring to join a club, the prospects still look bleak.

Gone are the days when you could breeze into the secretary's office, offer him a cigar, write out a cheque for the entrance fee and subscription and drift along to the 1st tee. The path to membership is strewn with all manner of obstacles and one false move can send you scurrying back to the 5 am tee time at the nearest municipal course.

The first barrier you have to overcome is the dreaded waiting list, which can extend from three years to infinity. The next is to find a proposer and a seconder for your application. These people have to be members of the club and usually need working on with generous offers of the odd case of vintage Bollinger, maybe a day out in your box at Ascot or a cruise around the Caribbean in your yacht.

Finally, if you progress this far you will be required to face the selection committee. The committee knows perfectly well that you have bought all the favours imaginable to reach this stage, but they just want to make sure you have bought them discreetly without being "flash".

In short, they want to ascertain that you are a "good chap", capable of getting it round in under 100, able to stand your turn in the bar afterwards, and unlikely to leg it over the horizon with the steward's nubile daughter.

But judging from some recent information, even getting on the waiting list is going to pose problems. It appears that some clubs are now interviewing applicants to see if they are suitable to join the waiting list. This, to my mind, creates all kinds of possibilities. It could herald the creation of a completely new sub-culture in golf.

Potential members would not be judged on their suitability as a golfer but whether they were appropriate waiting list material. Pretty soon the waiting list could develop into a club in its own right, with a captain, vice-captain, lady captain, committee and even a professional. Of course, waiting list golfers would have nowhere to play, but this wouldn't worry them – the main thing would be to have been accepted on the list.

Waiting list memberships could then be divided into categories – full, five-day, intermediate and so on. Subscriptions would be graded according to which category you belonged and there would be a substantial entrance fee.

The social cachet of actually belonging to a club would be replaced by waiting list oneupmanship. "I don't actually play that much old boy, but I've been accepted to the waiting list, you know."

The real bonus from all this would be that clubs would be able to virtually double their income without the extra strain on resources from people playing or using the club facilities. This money could then be used to help construct the extra 700 golf courses we need by the year 2000.
(1990)

Leaving a Divot in the Golf Course of Life

An item in my local newspaper the other day concerned the estate of a local businessman who bequeathed £500 for his pals to have drinks on him at his golf club in his memory.

It made me think about this whole business of leaving something behind for posterity when we hand in our final cards to the Great Recorder's Scoring Hut.

I've always felt that leaving a sum of money for one's cronies to become legless is probably the least memorable of these legacies. Once the money has been consumed, the only memory of your presence upon this earth is a cracking hangover and that's something most people want to forget. There is a compelling urge among golfers to leave something behind that perpetuates their name. Like most things in golf, there is a fairly strict pecking order as to how this is done, determined by how good you were as a player.

Thus, the really great players, as they are winding down their careers, embark on leaving the most permanent monument to their names in the shape of a golf course which they have designed. It is the ultimate ego-trip to shape an area of land according to your own personal preference.

The next stage down the line is the titled trophy. Again, there is a definite order which decides on to which kind of trophy your name can be attached.

At the top of the scale we have the international matches – Ryder, Walker, Curtis and Eisenhower, descending gradually through the various levels until we reach the ordinary club golfer.

Here we come across some of the more oddly named trophies, such as the Helen Brown Teapot or the Montrose Cleote Cup. If you don't consider yourself good enough to put your name on a trophy, then it seems the only path you can take is to request that your ashes are scattered somewhere on the course.

This can make you the butt of that very old joke about "the wind springing up and blowing you out of bounds again".

It's time a little more originality was encouraged in these final wishes. Henry Longhurst came up with a very good idea, which was to bequeath a tree which had to be planted in a specific place on the course. He then imagined future generations of golfers hacking about under its branches, pausing only to aim a kick at the plaque on the tree which carried his name.

My own preference would be to provide future players with a little more information on the tee. Alongside the length, par and stroke index of each hole, there should be room for some pithy comment about the hole. For example: Hole No 6, 473 yards, par 4, stroke index 1. "If you think you can get up here in two, think again" – C Plumridge.

Other members might wish to leave their comments, and over the years a broad picture of the hole would be built up, providing much more useful information than any diagram or yardage chart.

(1991)

PRIM, PROPER AND PROSPERING ON TRADITION

Despite the recession, on the Great Stock Exchange of Sport, golf is riding right up there among the Alpha Stocks. As in all markets, the reason for this is simply supply and demand. If a certain commodity is wanted by a great many people but there is not enough of that commodity to satisfy the need, then the price goes up in relation to the number of people who want it.

It may appear somewhat crude to put a price on what is, after all, a mere game, but the trend is to equate almost everything in terms of money because it is something to which we can all relate.

If we pursue the supply and demand theme further we come to the crux of the whole issue, and that is building more courses to cope with the rapidly increasing population who wish to slice, hook, top, shank and swear upon them.

Recognition of this need has now been made and it appears that every time you open a magazine or newspaper there are new plans afoot for yet another multi-million-pound complex that will feature everything from a bowling alley to a drive-in cinema as well as the normal "championship" course or two.

This is what worries me. At a dinner I attended during last year's Open Championship I fell into conversation with a visiting American. "If you belong to a country club in the States," he said, "you can play tennis, go swimming, exercise in the gymnasium, play badminton or fives, tackle a rubber or two of bridge, attend umpteen barbecues. But do you know the hardest thing to do? Finding a goddam game of golf!" In other words, he had seen the future and it wasn't working for golfers.

All these ancillary activities connected to the golf course are what lie ahead for us as new complexes spring up and the owners attempt to squeeze the last penny out of the users.

Of course, these sorts of places are not what I call proper golf clubs. They may call themselves golf clubs, but their glossy brochures, their effusive descriptions of the facilities and their general chromium-platedness leave them a long way from the real thing.

So how do you define a proper golf club? Well, it starts before you even get there because proper golf clubs are inordinately hard to find. "Just go down the A24, turn left on to the B33562, following that until you see Cherry Lane, ignore that, then turn right at the next crossroads, keep going for two miles and it's there on the left. You can't miss it." These instructions from your opponent tell you that when you do eventually arrive you will be well and truly on the trail of a proper golf club.

Proper golf clubs certainly do not have swimming pools, jacuzzis, saunas or beauty parlours for the ladies. They have locker rooms which carry a faint odour of floor polish, old socks and something unpleasant tucked away in the drying cupboard.

Ancient plumbing is a prerequisite of a proper golf club. Some proper golf clubs do have carpet tiles in the locker room but the majority stick to tiling or linoleum so you don't hang about and get into the bar quicker on a winter's day.

Proper golf clubs have a mixed lounge where the sexes can mingle freely but they also have a men's bar from which women are excluded except on high days and holidays.

The members of a proper golf club do not go round with their shirts unbuttoned to the waist with sundry gold ironmongery dangling round their necks. And that goes for the men as well.

If the members of a proper golf club happen to discuss professional golf, an occurrence which probably only crops up after the Open, they never refer to "Seve", "Nick", or "Woosie" but instead keep their relationships strictly on surname terms.

(1992)

Occupational Hazards

Browsing through last Tuesday's copy of the Daily Telegraph, I chanced across an article that immediately evoked a pang of asympathy.

Entitled "Physician Conceal Thyself" (full marks to the sub-editor who thought of that headline), it was written by a general practitioner who was outlining the essential need for a doctor to remain anonymous while taking the wife and kids away for a few weeks' holiday.

Dealing with upset stomachs in the Dordogne, stated the writer, was beyond his remit, and while his Hippocratic Oath occasionally created a deep moral dilemma, by and large he kept his occupation secret whenever he was away from home.

Being permanently on duty is not solely confined to medics – car mechanics, plumbers and even members of the clergy are all likely to be accosted socially in pubs or clubs or even in the local supermarket. To that list can also be added all golf correspondents.

After a day at a tournament spent trying to wring a story out of three players tied on 73, and not the slightest sign of a controversy in sight, the golf correspondent too may feel, and thoroughly deserve, a quiet drink away from the pressures of his work.

But it is at his peril that he enters any hostelry where he is known. "Hallo," will say a friendly voice, "I expect you've been at the golf. I saw some of it on the box at lunchtime.

"Tell me, what club did Ballesteros use for his second shot to the 14th? Couldn't have been more than a 7-iron I reckon, after that drive – still I expect you saw it in the flesh out there on the course. Dear me, what a life you chaps have!

"Who do you think is going to win? The highlights are on at 11.45 pm, you won't want to miss those, will you?"

The splintering sound that may be heard at this juncture is not to be taken seriously. It is only the golf correspondent chewing pieces from the rim of his glass.

What our friend doesn't realise is that after a day at a tournament, during which thousands of shots are struck, the significance of Ballesteros's second shot to the 14th tends to get lost in the general *mêlée*. Furthermore, the chances of us being in that precise spot at that particular moment are extremely remote. Lastly, having spent the day totally immersed in golf, the prospect of staying up until midnight to soak up some more via television is enough to have us swiftly committed.

For the great majority of these people, golf is a hobby totally removed from their work. But it is a hobby in which they can become completely obsessed.

It is, therefore, difficult for them to imagine it in any other context, even for someone whose job just happens to be in golf. But golf correspondents are human, too. When we are cut, do we not bleed?

Our views and interests are not totally centred on golf. We read Proust and Jeffrey Archer (mostly the latter), we listen to Puccini and Eric Clapton (mostly the former), we use our vote, carry our mortgages and pay our taxes.

Our tastes are catholic, but golf remains the overriding concern in our dealings with other people. The only refuge for us is when we are gathered together among ourselves.

Paradoxically, it is when we are all at a tournament that we can give free expression to our other interests, in the full knowledge that the one topic which will be hardly mentioned is golf. Although the Press Centre is the hub of information concerning the actual play, it provides us with sanctuary from incessant golf talk.

Ultimately, however, there is no getting away from it. After all, we have made our comfortable beds and we really don't mind the odd lump in the mattress.

Some years ago I recall talking with the South African professional Dale Hayes just before he was due to play in a pro-am. During the conversation I mentioned casually that I had just finished writing an instructional book aimed at those known to us all as beginners.

Having previously seen me play, Mr Hayes thought it highly amusing that I should presume to be telling other people how to play the game.

Later that day our paths crossed again. One of my approach shots had, rather unluckily I felt, finished behind an enormous chestnut tree.

As I stood, like the village blacksmith, under the tree's spreading branches, pondering my next stroke, Mr Hayes, accompanied by a sizeable gathering, walked over from an adjoining fairway.

He looked at my ball, he looked at the green, he looked at the tree and a beatific smile spread menacingly across his features. "Tell me," he inquired, "on what page of your instruction book is this particular shot featured?"

That was one occasion when I would rather have been a doctor. (1992)

SINGING FOR YOUR SUPPER

We are now entering the season of the golf club dinner and all over the country, club captains and various other dignitaries are standing in front of bathroom mirrors mouthing the words "unaccustomed as I am to public speaking".

This, of course, is the chief problem about many after-dinner speakers – they *are* unaccustomed to public speaking. It is only after the audience has sat through some turgid litany on the state of the greens and the refurbishment of the locker room plus the recounting of some dreadful old golfing joke that the listeners realise just how unaccustomed they are.

There are certain ground rules regarding after-dinner speaking, the most important of which is: keep it brief. Five minutes of straight, down the middle stuff will endear you far more to your audience than 25 minutes of rambling through the rough of your golfing memories.

Another golden rule is never preface a joke with the words "which reminds me of a story". This introduction warns the audience that you are about to tell a joke which they have, in all probability, heard before, and will certainly guarantee a lukewarm response. It is far better to work your stories into the text of your speech so that they arrive unexpectedly. But, by and large, unless you are an accomplished speaker it is best to avoid trying to be funny altogether.

Of all the golfing speeches that I have heard, and I've certainly heard a few, only three stand out. They were delivered by Henry Longhurst, Lord Deedes and John Wild, a former President of the English Golf Union. The first two were both journalists and had led such interesting and varied lives that one could have listened to them long after the last decanter of port had passed by. John Wild is not a journalist, but his account, delivered in flat Lancashire tones, of how he tried to persuade the R&A to stage the Open Championship at his home club of Wigan, is well worth catching if you have the opportunity.

For the golf correspondent attending a dinner, not as a speaker but as a guest, there are two pitfalls – being bored before dinner and being bored during dinner. Before dinner there is always the likelihood that you will be trapped in a corner by somebody who wishes to tell you what he thinks about the Ryder Cup, the Open Championship, his new swing and how he never reads your stuff anyway.

The best way to combat this individual is to utilise what is known as the diplomat's ploy. This involves arming yourself with two drinks so that when you are pinned to the wall by a crashing bore you can make your escape by saying: "I'd love to listen to you, but I really must take this drink over to my friend."

Being bored during dinner is another matter altogether since there is usually no escape. If you find yourself in this position you may care to adopt a system I devised while I was at school and was forced every Sunday to sit through the mandatory sermon by various visiting ecclesiastical bores.

The system worked on the basis that every time the Lord's name was mentioned it indicated a shot of true class and when the forces of darkness and evil were invoked a shot that was not so good. Thus, if the visiting churchman chose for his text "And the Lord said get thee behind me Satan" you were off the 1st with a good drive but missed the green with the second.

A course was selected according to the parish from which the priest came. On this basis, I once went round Little Aston with the then Bishop of Birmingham, a very devout man, in 62. Mind you, one particularly fiery Ulster clergyman cost me a 98 at Royal County Down.
(1990)

THE SPIDER'S LEGACY

It came to my notice last weekend that the bulk of the membership of my club was going to celebrate something called Burns' Night.

This apparently would take the form of an inedible meal being served for dinner to the accompaniment of loud, off-key music heralded by a speech in a totally unintelligible language.

Rumour had it that the evening was linked to the Scots and proved to me once again – such was the clamour for tickets – that there must be more Scots living outside Scotland than residing in it.

One is then left with the question as to why this is so. There are a number of reasons, not least being the weather, which makes certain parts of the country good places to emigrate from in search of milder climes. But any theories propounded on this subject must include golf.

The game appears to have motivated more Scots to travel to the far-flung corners of the globe than anything else. From the equatorial forests of Africa to the snowy wastes of the Antarctic, wherever two or three Scots are gathered together in the name of Tom Morris, then you can bet your last bawbee that before very long a golf course will be created and a club formed.

This missionary zeal is all very laudable, but those people of non-Scottish origin, particularly the English, should beware of the real intentions of these itinerant Celts.

Considering the hostility of some of the Scottish landscape upon which golf is played, it's not surprising that the Scots take golf extremely seriously. After all, a round at Carnoustie in a force-eight gale is no laughing matter.

Such conditions only confirm the Scots' belief that if God had meant golf to be enjoyable, then He would have made them play it in a more temperate climate on terrain more suited to its purpose. But courses such as Carnoustie and St Andrews are mere training grounds for the real business, which is, of course, revenge on the English.

The whole thing is rooted in history. The Scots have never forgotten Culloden and Flodden Field, where the English turned them over rather badly, and while the English should be smarting over their defeat at Bannockburn, they aren't.

Golf gives the Scots a recurring opportunity to avenge those crushing reversals of the past, which is why they infiltrate the clubs of England to try to satisfy their national lust for English scalps.

For example, at my club there is an annual England versus Scotland match among the members. Actually, the match should be renamed Scotland versus The English League since the English have to call upon representatives from many other nationalities to make an equivalent number with the proliferating Scots.

The atmosphere preceding this encounter epitomises the attitude of the Scottish golfer. The English and their co-opted team-mates arrive with tolerant smiles on their faces, indulging their opponents' little charade.

The Scots gather in a united clan, the tang of heather emanates from them like fog off a bog, their captain gives them a medicinal snort of whisky and, with a cry of "Get inty them", they all smash their glasses in the fireplace.

After the match there is a dinner, at which haggis is served to take away the taste of all the Scotch that is being drunk. Or is it the Scotch that takes away the taste of the haggis? Anyway, one follows the other in a ritual which leaves non-Scots with chronic indigestion.

Invariably, this dinner becomes a wake for the Scots and the pain of defeat can only be anaesthetised by imbibing large quantities of that amber fluid which bears their name. This is how the Scots have earned the reputation of being among the less abstemious of races.

What the Scots fail to realise is that they are outnumbered by the English, so by the law of averages there are more good English golfers than Scottish. Therefore, England is going to win more times than it loses.

It's no good the Scots thinking they are going to repeat their Bannockburn performance every time; there are just too many English around for that.

When Robert Bruce sat in his cave in 1314 watching the spider weaving busily, he completely misinterpreted its intention. Bruce thought the spider was telling him to keep battling on, but he was wrong.

The spider was really on a practice run for the biggest web of its life, so that it could catch all those English flies it knew would be following Edward II across the border.

While Bruce was deciding whether to play square-to-square, four-two-four or open with his seamers, the spider was acutely aware of the population difference and turning it to his advantage. Even in those days the spinner's craft was underrated.

(1987)

Playing Around

The Hole in the Road

There is a vague recollection lurking in the back of my mind concerning an enterprising American newspaper publisher who, sick of war, strikes, floods, rape, pestilence, famine and the other myriad horrors that filled his daily columns, decided he would publish a paper which contained nothing but good news. Within the week the paper had folded for the very simple reason that nobody bought it, thereby leaving the anguished publisher, who really should have known better, to reflect on the perversity of human nature. While the story is probably apocryphal, it nonetheless serves to illustrate the age-old principle that bad news attracts, a message that is revealed to us not only via the media but also in our everyday lives.

I remember standing behind the 13th green at Wentworth watching the final of last year's Colgate World Match-Play when, the players having holed out, the crowd dispersed and a large man wearing spiked golf shoes jumped down from one of those infernal ladders that spectators carry and landed with no small effect upon my left ankle. That story is thoroughly authenticated by the dull ache that even now pervades my left foot, but the point of telling it is that within seconds of my being pole-axed a reasonable crowd had gathered, some solicitous as to my well-being, others merely curious as to whether any of my regulation eight pints were staining the grass. The incident was not without humour for a few months earlier I had been summoned by a totally misguided captain to open the innings for the Association of Golf Writers in their annual cricket match against the touring golf professionals. The venue for this contest was no less a shrine than the Oval and again, it pains me to recall, I was felled by a sharp outswinger which struck me on, you've guessed it, the left ankle.

Back to Wentworth, and as I lay writhing on the ground I spat out through clenched teeth, "It's the same bloody ankle I was struck on at the Oval" – a remark that my colleague Norman Mair later reported as causing a by now respectful crowd to draw back, fearing perhaps that one of England's mainstays in the coming defence of the Ashes would not be able to make the trip to Australia.

The bad news theme is well-strummed in sport. Spectators gather at tortuous corners on Grand Prix racing circuits not to study the drivers' technique in negotiating the bend but in the hope that they will witness a multiple crash. In cricket, the sight of a bowler inflicting grievous bodily harm on a batsman rouses the crowd's blood lust to shout for more. Has not the popularity of the Grand National been founded on the well-orchestrated crunch of bone on gristle? The so-called noble art of boxing has its roots in the jungle and virtually every sporting contest is a throw-back to the days of the gladiators, when the combatants fought for the ultimate prize.

"Ah," I can hear you saying, "that may well be so, but we golf spectators are a civilised bunch, our game is free of physical contact, we are purists come to study at the university of immortals, such base behaviour is beneath us." Well, dear golf spectator, I am sorry to disillusion you. While it is true there is no real blood spilt during actual play, you too exhibit the perfectly natural human desire to be present at the scene of an accident.

There are many potential black spots on the world's golf courses and when the world's leading players set foot on such holes, the noise of the galleries can be likened to the squabbling of vultures awaiting their turn at the carcass. Among such holes could be listed the 12th at Augusta National, with its swirling winds waiting to push the ball back into Rae's Creek; the 17th at Carnoustie with the insidious Barry Burn snaking across the fairway; the 18th at Pebble Beach, where the Pacific Ocean washes away any stroke which has the hint of a hook. All of these examples have the ingredient of water in their sometimes indigestible recipe and there is nothing surer to gather the crowds than the presence of that particular element. The finality of a stroke which sends the ball plunging into unknown depths is a spectacle no self-respecting disaster-watcher can resist. But there is one hole in the world which, although without a water hazard, is truly the Becher's Brook of golf. It is probably the most famous hole in the world, located on certainly the most famous course.

The 461-yard, par four 17th at St Andrews, known universally as the Road Hole, has been drawing the metaphoric blood of golfers from the era of Tom Morris through to the era of Tom Watson. Some of its teeth have been pulled, the removal of the old railway sheds and the resurfacing of the road itself may have caused some spinning in the more notable graves up in the local churchyard, but even in this age of atomic golf balls and wonder-flex shafts, the Road Hole can still exact savage retribution.

The hole is a marvellous example of the use of angles to confuse and frustrate the golfer. From the tree, the presence of the out-of-bounds on the right instinctively draws the player's aim away to the left. But the further left the tee shot, the more imperceptible becomes the target of the green. And what a target. The front of the green rises alarmingly on to a narrow shelf and again, the angle of the green in relation to the approach shot means that any stroke slightly overhit will skitter through on to the dreaded road. That really should be enough but nature has conjured up one more impossible trick in the shape of the Road bunker on the left of the green, "eating its way into its very vitals", as Bernard Darwin once described it.

On such a stage have walked many players, some to rise to the challenge the Road Hole presents, others to suffer a severe mauling. It seems entirely appropriate that the hole played a major role in the achievements of Bobby Jones during his unsurpassable year of 1930. That year the Amateur Championship, a title Jones had never won, was held at St Andrews, and after some narrow escapes Jones found himself facing Cyril Tolley in the semi-finals. It proved to be one of the classic encounters of all time containing, as Jones wrote later: "the completely brutal ferocity of man-to-man contest". The pair arrived at the 17th all square, Tolley having won the 16th, and then came the stroke that provokes controversy even to this day. Jones's second shot struck a spectator standing at the back of the green and was, some people say, prevented from running on to the road. Other people present swear it would have stayed up anyway, but the upshot of it was that Jones halved the hole and went on to win the match at the 19th. The following day he easily disposed of Roger Wethered in the final to complete the first leg of his Impregnable Quadrilateral.

Although ifs count for nothing in golf, the question remains as to whether, if Jones's second had run on to the road, he would surely have lost the hole and perhaps the match and the first leg of his Grand Slam. Today there would be no cause for such conjecture over the fate of that shot for the crowd are kept back behind the wall beyond the road, leaving the ball to chart its own unfettered course.

Thirty years later in the Centenary Open Championship, the Road Hole proved to be the stumbling block in Arnold Palmer's quest for the title. He played the hole in four strokes more than the winner, Kel Nagle, and lost by one to the Australian. The hole is an anathema to Palmer for it goes against the very foundations of his attacking principles. Some 18 years after his debut at St Andrews, Palmer was still trying to bludgeon the Road Hole into submission when he was tied for the second-round lead in last year's Open

Championship. But again the hole won as Palmer drove out-of-bounds and took seven. "It's a good hole, a tough hole," said Palmer, "you have to play safe and I try to do something different every time and it just doesn't work. I try to make it a par four and I'm not really sure it is a par four." The next day Palmer again drove out-of-bounds for another seven.

The Road Hole also spread its malevolent influence beyond its boundaries for I am sure the reason Doug Sanders took five up in the 18th in the 1970 Open Championship was because he had escaped disaster on the 17th. His second shot to the 17th in the final round finished in the Road bunker, leaving him a splash shot of the utmost delicacy to a pin set tight to the hazard. Sanders executed the stroke brilliantly and his four was safe. Such was his relief that he even tempted fate by discarding his lucky tee peg for the drive up the last, feeling perhaps that nothing could prevent him from taking the title. Thus scorned, the fates wrought their revenge on Sanders' second putt.

A year later the Road Hole was part of a happier occasion as Britain won the Walker Cup for only the second time. David March clinched the victory with a marvellous second shot to the 17th which finished on the green and so enabled him to defeat his opponent and make Britain's position impregnable.

And so we come to last year's Open Championship and once again the Road Hole played the major role in the outcome. The hole played to an overall average of 4.8 strokes throughout the Championship and there were just seven birdies gleaned by the world's best players. The highest score was nine, taken by Japan's Tsuneyuki Nakajima, who was on the green in two, putted into the Road bunker and took four to get out. That completed an unenviable double for Nakajima – the previous April he took 13 on the 13th at Augusta in the US Masters.

Only Ben Crenshaw tamed the Road Hole in that Open, recording three pars and a birdie, and even Jack Nicklaus had to be content with three fives and a four. Nicklaus played the hole as a par five, hoping to get his second shot up the crest and on to the flat portion of the green. "If it doesn't make the top," said Nicklaus, "you're still better off there than in the Road bunker or left of the bunker where you have no chance at all." In his final round Nicklaus stuck to his game plan and from below that mountainous approach struck one of the greatest long putts ever witnessed to within one foot of the hole.

Another casualty was Severiano Ballesteros who, two strokes ahead of the field in the second round, drove hugely out-of-bounds down the 17th. From his second drive, he struck a memorable 4-iron which pitched just over the Road bunker and stayed on the green, but it still meant a six for the Spaniard and he was never a factor from there on.

Ballesteros regards the hole in much the same way as Palmer, whose attacking instincts he has inherited. "I think maybe it is the most difficult hole I ever play," said Ballesteros in his broken English, "the way they put the flag I think maybe one day they put the flag on the road instead of the green." Should that unlikely event ever occur, there is no doubt in my mind that Ballesteros would still go for it, for the challenge of the Road Hole, like the Old Course itself, is eternal.

(1979)

IS IT TRUE WHAT THEY SAY ABOUT AUGUSTA?

Even if you are an itinerant golf writer, possessed of a fair degree of low animal cunning, standing on the 1st tee of Augusta National Golf Club you don't want to come up with an air shot.

Even if you are partnered by Joe, Jerry and Dick from Des Moines and it's the Monday morning after the epic Watson-Nicklaus chase of 1977, you still cannot shake off that tight feeling in your stomach.

Even if the only people watching are a fellow journalist come to jeer and those busy packing up the hot dog stands, you will find your lips moving in a silent plea to the Almighty that He, for once, will allow you to make reasonable contact with the ball.

Some people say waiting to drive off that 1st tee is the world's best laxative, but I'll just have to take their word for that. When you arrive at the course and are told you are on the tee in five minutes, you don't have too much time to think.

You just grab a caddie named George, run to the tee, put a ball down and hit it to the brow of the hill. Maybe that's the best way to avoid the butterflies and the frantic prayers.

It's the history that gets to you; all those immortal names, all those azaleas and dogwoods; all those breathtakingly beautiful holes, all wrapped up in the legend that was Bobby Jones and is now the legend of the US Masters.

After a week of watching the Masters won and lost, it's easy to fall into the trap of thinking that maybe this course is not quite all it's cracked up to be. You see so many superlative shots, so many birdies, so many putts dropped – all with apparent ease – that you tend to forget the problems the players have to face.

That illusion is dispelled the moment you walk on to the 1st green, sight down a putt with more turns than a corkscrew and, with a touch as light as your nerves will allow, send the ball six feet past the hole. Even though you hole the return, you cannot believe a green could be so fast. You still cannot believe it after two good shots down the 555-yard 2nd, when your pitch lands by the pin and bounds on to the back fringe.

Tom Weiskopf thinks of the 3rd as a second-shot hole played from the right side of the fairway. If your drive is left, he maintains, the pitch to this 360-yard hole will kick away to the right, leaving an impossible downhill putt across a table-top green, a putt that can accelerate right off the green into a bunker. Weiskopf was correct: you don't want to be on the right side of this green, but he's never had to calculate for the rank ineptness of this correspondent, who thinned an 8-iron along the ground and up the fronting ridge to within 15 feet of the hole. Two putts later it was three straight pars and eat your heart out Ben Hogan.

Jack Nicklaus maintains that the 220-yard 4th hole plays shorter than it looks and a great many inexperienced players think it's a wood from the tee. Even from the middle tee, some 20 yards nearer, it looks a long way. When you see your shot with a four wood finishing over the back of the green and nearly out of bounds, you get the feeling that Nicklaus knows a little more than you. But then he's had plenty of Masters to find out.

Hardly anyone goes to the 5th, which is set high on a ridge above the main action below. This lack of attention resulted in three putts from what seemed infinity with two levels. The short 6th is where Billy Joe Patton, the American amateur, holed in one in 1954 during his chase of Hogan and Snead. It was also where, in 1974, Art Wall completed his run of three consecutive twos. This British amateur was happy with his par.

The idea on the 365-yard 7th is to drive it straight down the funnel of trees and flip a short iron up on to the green lying above you. There is another way to play it, and that is to hit a high, looping hook over the trees and then hit an 8-iron to the green. What you mustn't do is put your second above the hole, because the downhill putt will mean you'll three putt just like I did.

Slog it all the way uphill on the 530-yard 8th and then start the downhill run to the 440-yard 9th, where you're certain to be going into the green with a long iron from a trapeze. That's the first nine and the best is yet to come. Can the nerves stand up or will the heat get you first?

The 10th is 485 yards long and just beautiful. Called the "Cathedral of Pines" because of the giant sentinels that surround the green, this hole requires a draw from the tee to reach the flatland at the bottom and shorten the approach. The second is then played over an artistic splash of sculptured bunkers to a green with the softness of cement.

Ray Floyd, joint Masters record-holder with Nicklaus, likes to keep his drive on the 445-yard 11th down the left side. He wants his drive there so he's hitting his second across the water that flanks the left side of the green. Gary Player also favours this approach, but Doug Ford, winner in 1957, banked on a drive down the centre and a hooked second which he aimed to bounce off the banking right of the green.

So much has been written, said and sworn about the 155-yard 12th, that when you stand on the tee all the stories come flooding back to confuse you. You remember hearing that the worst place to be is in one of the bunkers at the back of the green because then you're blasting out from a downhill lie towards Rae's Creek. You remember reading about the dogwood tree on the right of the green and that if it's moving, the wind is blowing.

You remember all this folklore and, when you've taken five different clubs out of your bag, you finally keep one and swing on another prayer. Up it goes and you watch. The dogwood tree is moving and it's going to be short – no it's not, it's too long. Glory be, it's on the back fringe and two putts later you have your three, which feels like a minus two.

You play the 485-yard par five 13th as a par five unless you're one off the pace in the Masters. Otherwise, you lay up short of the creek that meanders in front of the green and you pitch up to a pin that is so tight to the edge of the ditch it seems almost afloat.

So it's amen to Amen Corner and on to the 420-yard 14th, with its rolling green. The rule here is to be at the back of the green with the second shot.

When you reach the 15th you remember you have seen it on television, but it never looked like this. Drive to the crest of the hill and think of Gene Sarazen and the 1935 albatross. No wonder the cameras cluster here, waiting hopefully for a repeat performance.

The professionals always try to go for the green over the water, because to lay up means facing, as Nicklaus says, the "toughest pitch in golf" from a downhill lie to a front of green pin position. If, like me, you hit a fat, 4-iron second when your caddie's telling you it's only a 6-iron to lay up, then you too will face the toughest pitch in golf. Get it anywhere on the green and give thanks.

Bath time awaits on the beautiful, scenic 190-yard chocolate box 16th. Water all the way between you and the green, which tends to make the hole appear shorter than it is. Don't fall into that trap. Hit a 4-wood all the way and to hell with the pros hitting a 6-iron. Remember that the 17th, at 400 yards, plays longer than it looks. Take a club more for the second shot and, when you three-putt for the sixth time, just reckon that's about par.

The 18th is only one of two holes at Augusta that doglegs to the right (the other is the 1st). It's 420 yards long and uphill all the way. By now you're drained by the heat but you manage to get the drive away reasonably. George hands you that old 4-wood and tells you to hit it right on the pin, which you can just see above the big deep bunker on the left of the green.

You hit it straight into that bunker and George rolls his eyes heavenwards, muttering about a dumb sonofabitch who can't hit it where he's told. You are in the very same bunker Jack Nicklaus found himself in the day before. He, you may remember, failed to get down in two and that was the end of his chase of Tom Watson. It's the first bunker you've been in, which isn't so surprising as there are only 44 on the entire course.

The sand is firm, but powdery underneath. If you dig too deep your club may come out in Vladivostok. Keep the club low and hit right through. Up she pops and nearly goes into the hole. Hey Jack, where are you?

And so the walk over hallowed ground has finished; the communion with the saints has passed. Was that Horton Smith who brushed by me as I chipped at the 4th? Could that brightly clad figure behind the 7th green have been Jimmy Demaret? Was that Byron Nelson standing by the bridge across Rae's Creek at the 12th?

There was a man by the 16th green hitching up his trousers; could it have been Arnold Palmer? Was that soberly-dressed man on the 10th Ben Hogan? It could have been because he didn't say much. All those names, all those memories are with you during a round at Augusta National and the course brings them sharply into focus.

Is it true what they say about Augusta? Believe me, it is. In spades. (1977)

A DISCORDANT ROUND WITH RACHMANINOV

A few years ago I read about a man who claimed to be Britain's most accident-prone citizen. The catalogue of disasters for this former bus driver included five car crashes, four bus breakdowns, being knocked down by a motorbike, falling into a river and walking into a plate-glass door. These misfortunes resulted in him writing his autobiography, entitled *The Walking Disaster*. But I believe that sales were, well, disastrous.

Disaster is a permanent companion of anyone who sets foot on the golf links, but the subject of this discussion is not the disasters which befall us in terms of our score, but those players who are accidents looking for somewhere to happen.

These Golfing Disasters (GDs) are pretty rare birds, but occasionally, if you are unlucky enough, you come across one. GDs come to play golf but leave their brain elsewhere. Their occupations are often cerebral – an atom physicist, for example, a musician or even a writer – so, although they go through the motions of playing the game, their minds are dwelling on something entirely different.

GDs are fairly well camouflaged but can be identified. They often eschew modern golf clothing – shirts with stylish motifs are not in their wardrobe. Trousers are trousers, whether worn for work, gardening or experimenting in the laboratory, and the pair they wear for golf have been used for all these endeavours. Shoes are of the stout walking variety, converted by the hammering in of a few spikes.

Their equipment comprises a mixture of steel and hickory-shafted clubs contained in an old canvas bag. The whipping on the woods flutters in the breeze before becoming entangled with the irons, so that each time a club is selected, a tug of war develops which usually ends up with the entire set being ejected.

GDs always have their clubs on a trolley. In fact, this is the most dangerous part of their armoury because they are in possession of something which moves. First, they wedge their clubs firmly in the cleft of the trolley. This means that, in conjunction with the tangled whipping, club selection becomes a form of unarmed combat in which trolley, clubs and golfer end up on the ground in a chaotic mess.

Second, immediately the GD takes his trolley off the fairway, the trolley tilts and the bag falls off. Third, you can guarantee that when a GD eventually reaches the green, he invariably parks his trolley at the furthest point from the next tee.

GDs have absolutely no idea where their ball has gone after they have hit it. They labour under the illusion that each drive has travelled 100 yards further than it actually has. Even though you may tell them that their ball is halfway up a sand dune 50 yards from the tee, they walk steadfastly past it up the fairway. You then have to return with them to look for their ball and, once in the sand dune, the bag falls off the trolley.

My first experience with one of this species occurred many years ago in an autumn meeting. There were three of us, a former Oxford Blue, myself and the

GD, who arrived in a long-sleeved shirt with the cufflinks still in place and wearing crumpled grey trousers. He informed us that he had taken up golf to relax him from the cares of his profession as a concert pianist.

As we walked up the 1st fairway he started humming the first movement from Rachmaninov's Second Piano Concerto. Now I am as fond of Rachmaninov as the next man, but not at the top of my backswing. Two collapsed trolleys later we arrived at the third hole, where the Oxford Blue sent his second shot deep into the woods.

He then dropped another ball and planted it two feet from the hole. The GD suddenly shot off into the undergrowth and emerged triumphantly holding the original ball aloft. After a heated exchange, the Blue returned to the original spot, put the ball in a bunker, got it out and, visibly shaken, three-putted for an eight.

There were a number of last straws during the rest of the round, but the one which finally broke us occurred during the opening bars of Beethoven's Emperor, when the GD was asked to attend the flag stick and did so with his feet firmly placed across the line of my putt. Something snapped, and after further remonstrations the GD was shown the red card and left the course.

My most recent contact with a GD occurred a few months ago. Perhaps the two air shots on the 1st tee should have warned me I was in the presence of someone special. But to err is human, and all that.

As the round progressed, however, all the symptoms were evident – inability to see where the ball went, struggles with clubs on trolley, bag falling off trolley at regular intervals. It was a CD (Complete Disaster).

So be warned – there is one of them out there waiting to happen, and if you are not careful, he could happen to you.

(1985)

OVER THE TOP IN CLUB SELECTION

The vanity of man, it is said, knows no bounds, and perhaps nowhere is this more clearly evident than on the golf course. Here we find captains of industry making the kind of decision that, if practised in the boardroom, would ensure summary dismissal.

Apart from the obvious follies committed every day, such as taking a wood from thick rough, I would suspect the most frequent examples of the vanity syndrome occur at short holes.

This was brought home to me the other day while playing at my own club with a low-handicap friend. On the 165-yard 5th hole my friend was staggered when his 5-iron shot only just cleared the fronting bunkers, leaving him with a 30-yard chip shot to a pin set at the back of the green. "I don't believe it," he said. "I've never hit more than a 5-iron on this hole."

The fact we were hitting into a strong wind and that his type of shot was invariably of a high-soaring trajectory that settled quickly on landing did not seem to occur to him – he had always hit a 5-iron so why should today be any different?

Age and diminishing ability have long since taught me that it doesn't matter what club you hit at a short hole as long as it's enough club to get you there. The majority of short holes are designed with all the trouble at the front. It is far better to be long than just creeping on to the green, with the danger of not quite catching the shot and falling back.

I have one golden rule for all shots to the flag and it particularly applies to short holes: always take the club that will send the ball *over the top of the flag*. I don't know where I heard it, but for the normal standard of club golfer it is an invaluable maxim.

If you can visualise the ball flying over the top of the flag and take the club that will provide you with that distance, you will be surprised at the number of shots which finish level with the hole and how few finish past it.

Very few of us are like the professionals in that we know almost to the nearest yard how far we hit each club.

The variation in, say, just two shots with the same club may be anything up to 20 yards. Therefore, we should make allowances for these variations and always go over the top of the flag.

Of course, the other factor which confuses us in club selection is the fact that we have so many weapons from which to choose. How much easier it would be if, for example, we only carried the odd-numbered clubs.

Certainly we would not be caught out like Johnny Miller in the 1975 US Masters. After a first round of 75 he complained that his tee shots had left him "in between clubs".

Such absurdities would be removed with a limited choice before us, as would many of the doubts over whether we had the right club or not. If it's the only club in the bag capable of hitting the ball over the top of the flag it has to be the right one, doesn't it?

One of my favourite stories on this theme concerns a short-hitting lady golfer playing at Royal Troon who, on arriving at the 126-yard 8th hole (the Postage Stamp), was handed a driver by her caddie.

She hit the ball into one of the cavernous bunkers in front of the green, turned to the caddie and screamed: "Caddie, you underclubbed me!" (1990)

NEEDLES AND PINS

When it comes to the real blood and guts of golf there is no substitute for match-play. This is true gladiatorial stuff, a contest in which there has to be a winner and a loser, and no excuses afterwards can alter the result.

By comparison, stroke-play is numerical tedium where the final total is invariably depressingly high and always leaves behind the feeling that the score would have been a great deal better, if only...

As a regular perpetrator of what is known as war-time golf – out in 39, back in 45 – match-play has always been my preference. Indeed, it is the form of golf that the majority of golfers play most of the time.

The art of match-play lies as much in knowing when to go for the flag as when not to go for it; in being able to strike the telling shot at the right time and, hardest of all, the ability to cope with the sheer physical presence of your opponent standing at your shoulder on tee and green.

It is at this point we enter the dark realms of psychology and its bearing on the outcome of a match.

There is no doubt that the mind controls the destiny of a golfer and it is in match-play that this most delicately balanced organism is at its most perplexing and its most vulnerable.

History does not reveal who the first player was to exploit this weakness and even today it is hard to find a player who will admit to using what is commonly referred to as "the needle". Conversely, it is manifestly easy to find players who will recount when and how "the needle" was used on them!

Examples of such gamesmanship are numerous. In his marvellous book *The Education of a Golfer*, Sam Snead tells how he was needled out of the 1947 US Open title in the play-off with Lew Worsham.

After 17 holes the two were still tied and on the 18th both lay approximately the same distance from the hole in three strokes. Snead felt it was his turn to putt but, as he settled over the ball, Worsham stepped forward and said it was in fact his turn first.

When the distances were measured officially, Snead's ball was found to be further away, but by then his concentration had been broken and, naturally, he missed the putt. Worsham holed his to deny Snead the one major title he never won.

That is pretty crude stuff actually, and the true gamesman would never stoop so low. But a seemingly innocent remark or a shake of the head can be just as effective. For example, the true gamesman, on approaching a hole with an out-of-bounds, would never say: "You've got to watch the out-of-bounds here, old chap."

Instead, he would stand on the tee and survey the scene for some time before remarking: "Interesting how the architect left that tree there to keep you away from the boundary fence."

The words "tree" and "boundary fence" should be more than enough to conjure up visions of jungles and wild beasts, and cause the opponent to aim so far away from them that his ball will vanish deep into the woods on the other side.

Another useful gambit can be used on the green when your opponent has a long putt and you are considerably closer to the hole and well away from his line. As your opponent prepares to putt you ask politely if you should mark your ball, even though quite clearly it is nowhere near his line of sight.

Your opponent is nonplussed by the stupidity of your suggestion and, rightly, tells you curtly not to bother. His concentration, however, has been irrevocably broken because he is wondering what prompted you to ask such a damn fool question.

Of course, I have never resorted to such tactics myself but they have been used on me on numerous and memorable occasions. One in particular stands out because it was perpetrated by a notable golf correspondent, and not the sort of thing one expects from such a pillar of golfing society.

We were playing in some competition together and on one hole I had a medium length putt for a par. In going for it I knocked the ball a couple of feet past the hole. "Go on," said the man, who was supposed to be my friend, "just knock it in."

Before I had time to think, I had missed the one back and as I missed it I realised I had been well and truly "done", taken in by a classic lure. We have often laughed about it since, which just goes to show what a generous, forgiving soul I am.

The only disturbing thing about the entire episode is that had I taken my time over that second putt, marked the ball, looked at the line from both sides, peered at the edge of the hole to determine which way the grass was growing, it is just as likely that I would have still missed it anyway.

(1987)

WISH YOU WERE HERE

This is the time of year when most people, with the notable exception of golf correspondents, take their annual holidays. If they are golfers they will ensure that their holiday venue will be located near a course, a good watering hole and some decent weather.

In the past, this combination has meant hiking off abroad to somewhere like Spain or Portugal. Even if you can depart this sceptr'd isle without being baulked by air traffic controllers and harbourmasters, that is only part of the equation.

Once you arrive at your destination there's the chance that the food might be a little dodgy, the water undrinkable and the hotel room faces directly into another hotel room instead of the beach that you requested and hardly anybody speaks English. Worse still, when you arrive at the golf course all the starting times have been taken.

The obvious solution to this nightmare is to stay here, but this decision then begs the next question: namely, where to go in Britain?

There is a little oasis of sanity tucked away on the north coast of Cornwall. It's called Trevose, but don't let on I told you about it, otherwise I'll be lynched the next time I visit.

The people who go to Trevose are very protective about the place. They like to keep it for themselves because it represents one of the last bastions of civilised holiday golf in the western world.

The atmosphere is rather like the Halford Hewitt, but with fewer clothes. The golfers at Trevose do not open their shirts to the navel to display several tons of gold ironmongery on their chests.

Trevose is what I call proper holiday golf. You can go out in the evening for nine holes with a few clubs tucked in an old canvas bag and, with the sun glinting off the distant ocean, know that Harry Vardon is in his heaven and all's right with the world.

Golf has always been a part of my holidays. In the old days, a week in Bournemouth taking in Parkstone, Broadstone, Ferndown and Meyrick Park could be followed by another week in Suffolk and Norfolk taking in Aldeburgh, Thorpeness, Hunstanton, Brancaster, Sheringham and Cromer.

There was the feast of Lancashire with Royal Birkdale, Royal Lytham, Hillside, Formby and Southport & Ainsdale.

But best of all was Scotland. This was a time when petrol was 3/6d a gallon and you could get on to Muirfield for around £1 plus a sworn affidavit as to your character from the Archbishop of Canterbury.

It was a time when Gleneagles never looked more enticing and you could play St Andrews for a week without encountering one Japanese four-ball. You could play Troon in the morning, hit the Postage Stamp with your tee shot, finish the round in two hours and drive to Turnberry for the afternoon. You could wake up to the best breakfast in the world, play Carnoustie four times in a day and dance the night away with Miss Broughty Ferry.

I doubt if you can do any of these things now because golf has changed. I mourn the passing of my old canvas bag with its motley collection of clubs, one of which, an old hickory-shafted niblick, could make the ball sit up and beg. I dislike the use of yardage charts by club golfers; I believe that the maximum number of clubs allowed should be 10 and my views on coloured golf balls are well known.

Holiday golf is the ideal way to return to the game's original intentions. You can use the modern equivalent of the canvas bag, you can rely on judgement and feel for distance to execute a shot properly; you can even exhume your old hickory-shafted niblick if you like because holiday golf is all about having fun. Wish you were here.
(1982)

THE FAIREST OF ALL

Of all the great links courses upon which championships are housed, none provides a fairer challenge than Muirfield, which this week stages the Amateur Championship for the ninth time.

The essence of Muirfield is its open aspect. There is none of the secrecy that abounds on links shrouded by dunes, where desolate scrubland disappears into some distant horizon. Muirfield is straight and honest, a course where the player can see what he has to do – the only criterion is the ability to do it.

Quite apart from its playing qualities, Muirfield is a great "watching" course. Here, the spectator does not set out from the 1st tee knowing that the sanctuary of the clubhouse will not reappear until the 18th green. Instead, the watcher is presented with an abundance of alternatives. The only agony lies in the decision.

Should one walk the first three holes and then cut across to the 15th fairway and take in the last four? Or perhaps a walk down to the 10th green will prove fruitful as, from there, one can watch the drives from the 8th tee, view the distant 6th green and the whole of the short 7th.

The discerning spectator will, however, have no hesitation in retracing his steps to the ridge which crosses the front of the 11th tee. From here can be seen the remainder of the 11th with the 5th green beyond, the entire length of the 12th and, if the watcher turns about, the teeshots to both the 13th and 14th come into sight. Viewed from this vantage point, the golf may become secondary as the compelling vista of the Firth of Forth rivets the eye – a silver stretch of water which may be twinkling in the sunshine or laden with a mist through which one can picture a dirty British coaster with a salt-caked smoke stack.

Yet for all its beauty Muirfield can be a lonely place. It was here that Bobby Jones was beaten in the quarter-finals of the 1926 Amateur Championship when it seemed he would carry all before him. In an evocative piece of writing by O B Keeler, who acted as Boswell to Jones's Johnson, the pain of that defeat was memorably isolated. "In all my life I have never heard of anything as lonely as the cry of the peewit in that twilight of the rolling Muirfield course, nor was I ever so lonesome."

The period between the wars was undoubtedly the golden age of amateur golf. In addition to Jones, the Dark Blue trio of Cyril Tolley, Ernest Holderness and Roger Wethered all put their names on the trophy. To have been a gentleman amateur golfer at that time must have been idyllic.

After the Second World War, the names of Joe Carr and Michael Bonallack became synonymous with the amateur ethos but already the picture was changing. Improved prize money among the professionals meant that there were fewer amateurs establishing themselves in the public eye before they were lost in the lower echelons of the paid ranks.

Now amateur golf has become merely a training ground for future professionals: but victory in the Amateur is far from being an indication of professional success. Since 1980, eight winners have turned professional and of these only José Maria Olazabal has made a real impact.

The 1980 winner, Duncan Evans, who worked in the family fish and chip business, turned professional but the fire of the paid ranks caused him to return to the frying pan from which he had jumped. The 1982 champion, Martin Thompson, also became reinstated as an amateur; Philip Parkin has struggled, David Curry has yet to win his player's card, Paul Mayo finished 171st on the money list last year and the 1988 champion, Christian Hardin, hasn't surfaced at all.

These portents have failed to discourage last year's winner, Stephen Dodd, from travelling down the same potholed road, and one can only wish him well.

His defection plus the absence of Peter McEvoy and Garth McGimpsey means that a new name will appear on the trophy since there are no former champions in the draw.

Meanwhile, let us be content with our view from the ridge of the 11th, a gentle wind, the waters of the estuary, the trees of Archerfield Wood standing dark and forbidding on the eastern side while, above us, the lark's exultant song signals our own rhapsody at being in such a place.
(1990)

WELL, I'M BUGGED

For all the breakthroughs in modern medicine I suppose the one that has most benefited golfers is the replacement hip job. In the past golfers with atrophying hip joints faced the bleak prospect of hanging up their clubs for good; now they can be given a new lease and continue playing until the Great Starter finally calls their name.

Such is the demand for the operation, however, there is a waiting list which can extend to two years and beyond. During this period sufferers find they have either to curtail their golf or seek alternative means of getting round the course. If they wish to carry on playing then the only means of transport is a golf buggy.

These machines have proved a great boon to the aged and infirm, and many enlightened clubs have allowed their afflicted members to use them. However, it has come to my notice that a club in Cheshire has run into the sort of problem which only seems to occur in British golf clubs.

The situation arose when the club decided to allow the use of buggies for four of its members, one of whom was the club President. Everything was running smoothly until one of the buggy users made the mistake of winning a major competition. "Unfair!" cried the opposition and, after a committee meeting, it was decided that buggies would not be allowed for competitions.

Far be it from me to tell this club how to manage its affairs, but it would appear that an element of jealousy may well have crept in. If buggy users have a need for their machine then surely they are disadvantaged anyway? The benefits of a buggy are purely in providing mobility; apart from that they can be a positive handicap.

First of all, they destroy the rhythm of a round insofar as once you have hit a shot you find yourself arriving at the ball in no time at all, ready to hit the next one. When you are walking round you have time to assess the lie of the land, the direction of the wind and how these would affect your next shot. Golf from a buggy is a high-speed exercise where you have to concentrate on steering the thing and stay ready to cut the engine when your playing companions are about to hit a shot. I would go so far as to say that because of these factors a buggy user's handicap should be increased by two shots under Rule 19!

My first experience with a buggy occurred inevitably in the land of the free drop and the cart path. I was staying at a resort course in Florida and, awakening very early one morning, felt that a few holes before breakfast would be just the ticket. It was a beautiful day and I had just driven my ball from the 2nd tee when the peace and tranquillity was suddenly shattered. From out of the undergrowth emerged a buggy driven by what I can only describe as a latterday version of Simon Legree.

Large, ruddy faced and with a neck in the Gareth Chilcott mould, it was a uniformed course ranger, complete with a ten-gallon hat and a rather menacing looking gun strapped to his side. He pulled up beside me, "What do you think you're doing, boy?" I gave him the full Bertie Wooster. "Splendid morning," I replied, "sun shining, birds doing their stuff, all nature crying fore, couldn't be better."

"Don't get smart with me, boy," he growled. "Just get your ass back to the clubhouse and hire yurself a golf cart. Ain't no walking round here." Realising there was no point in arguing, I trudged back to the clubhouse, paid $35 for a cart and discovered how to play mechanised polo.

So the buggy is here to stay with more and more of them buzzing round our courses; especially when you consider the rise in the average age of the British golfer and the number of new hips that will entail.
(1992)

FOUR-FOOTED FRIENDS OR FOES?

I tend to be circumspect in my approach to dogs. Various canine clashes in the past have taught me that other people's dogs can be unpredictable in response to any gestures of affection, and I have the scars to prove it.

As a child, I can remember my parents owning just one dog. It was a sort of Jack Russell which had run to fat and went by the name of Nutty. This was appropriate since the animal was definitely certifiable and its whole existence was based on the philosophy of "if it moves, bite it". This meant that anyone or anything passing by our house galvanised Nutty into a headlong attack and, judging by the agonised cries which followed, his bite was far worse than his bark.

Fortunately for our standing in the neighbourhood, Nutty found it difficult to discriminate between those targets which were soft and yielding and those which were not. Thus it was that he met a timely end while attempting to take a chunk out of a passing lorry, and his passing was mourned by no one.

There are doubtless many golfers who own dogs and are therefore able to use taking the dog for a walk as an excuse for getting in a few holes. Many dog-owning golfers bring their animals with them when they are about to engage in a match, and this is when the art of dogmanship comes into play.

Most dogs accompanying their owners are perfectly well behaved, sitting quietly by their master's bag before walking quietly at heel. Others, even better trained perhaps, adopt a crouching position by the tee and, just as the opponent is at the top of the swing, dart off in pursuit of the ball in a most distracting fashion. Some dogs, when released from the lead, track down the scent of their master's ball and nudge it into a favourable lie, and then go on to track down the scent of my ball and nudge it into an old divot hole.

This latter aspect of dogmanship may strike you as unlikely, but I can assure you it happened to me on several occasions while on holiday at Trevose in Cornwall. The owners will know exactly what I am talking about.

Generally speaking, dogs on the golf course are an infernal nuisance, but they do have one constructive function. They are wonderful ball detectors. I remember as a lad not long after the war, when golf balls were far less expendable than they are now, accompanying a neighbour and her dog on to the course. The dog, a springer spaniel, would average about 12 balls on a reasonable walk and, since the lady herself was a golfer, she knew exactly where to look.

The thicket to the right of the 4th tee was a particularly fruitful area since it was blind from the tee and could be guaranteed to yield up half a dozen balls in varying conditions, and not one delivered with a tooth mark on it. Since I used to receive a reasonable percentage of these finds, I shouldn't complain too much.

The finding of balls in this manner appeals to that instinct in all of us of getting something for nothing. Whether there are any legal implications in this I'm not sure, but I would make the proviso that lost balls are fair game only to dog-owning *members*. There is nothing more infuriating, having lost a ball, to find on your next outing some grubby little urchin, accompanied by an equally scruffy dog, offering to sell you your own ball.

A recent incident at my home club confirmed what I have felt all along about dogs on the golf course. On the short 11th I struck a 4-iron towards the green, whereupon, due to circumstances completely beyond my control, the ball took it upon itself to veer violently to the left, perilously close to the out-of-bounds fence.

On arriving at my ball I found that it was in bounds, but had come to rest slap in the middle of a large and recent dog deposit. A number of rules sprang to mind. Was the obstruction a loose impediment? A closer look revealed that it may have been an impediment, but it certainly wasn't loose.

Was it an immovable obstruction? No, but I wasn't going to be the one to move it. I knew of course that it was against the rules to play a ball in a motion so in the end I removed the ball, took a penalty drop and proceeded.

Looking back I am sure I could have taken relief under rule 19-1A, which covers a ball coming to rest in any moving or animate outside agency. Although the obstruction was inanimate to the eye, chemical analysis would have revealed it to be positively seething with life.

Anyway, from now on I am going to call my 4-iron "Stanley". Why? Simply because it was another fine mess it had got me into.
(1990)

CAMPAIGN TRAIL

THROWING IN THE TOWEL

We are often informed that the Rules of Golf mean exactly what they say and are written to give a clear and succinct answer to the multitude of circumstances which are created by the application of club to ball.

Ignorance or misinterpretation of the rules are the commonest reasons for any breaches that occur and most of us have to find out the hard way if we have transgressed. Professional golfers are more blessed, since at tournaments there are a host of officials present to advise and consult with before taking any irrevocable steps. Officials, however, are only human and sometimes even they make mistakes but a recent incident on the US Tour demonstrates that an over-zealous application of the rules is sometimes misplaced.

The incident in question involved Craig Stadler, who was playing in the third round of the San Diego Open. On the 14th, Stadler put a drive under a tree and the only way he could make a swing at the ball was to get down on his knees. This supplicatory action is not actually covered by the rules since Rule 13-3: "Building Stance" states that a player is entitled to place his feet firmly in taking his stance but he shall not build a stance. No mention of knees there, and since such a position would only leave the toes of the feet touching the ground this could be regarded as a non-stance. But many players have knelt down to play a shot without being penalised and Stadler could draw on these precedents.

It was what happened next that caused the controversy. The area around Stadler's ball was extremely muddy and as he didn't want to ruin the pretty pastel shades of his slacks, he put down his golf towel to kneel on while making the shot. He played the shot and went on his way with his trousers unsullied. Nobody thought any more of it until the incident was reported by someone who had seen it on TV.

At this stage Stadler had completed the tournament, finishing in joint second place for a handy cheque of $37,500. Now the US Tour officials stepped in. While it was all right for Stadler to kneel down, it was not all right for him to place a rolled up towel on the ground to kneel upon. Indeed, the US Tour had in fact answered this specific point earlier in the season and therefore, according to the Tour's interpretation of the rule, Stadler was completing a stance. He was then disqualified and forfeited the 37,500 smackers.

The first point to arise from this is how could Stadler be building a stance when he hadn't actually taken a proper stance in the first place? The second point, and one which has arisen before, is should retrospective action be taken as the result of televised coverage? And the third point is, haven't the US Tour officials put their feet right in the mire by taking this action? The US Tour spokesman stated that a golf towel was as much a piece of a player's equipment as a golf bag and laying down the golf bag to provide a line for a shot was illegal, so it was therefore illegal to lay down a towel. Since there were no officials present at the time, have they evidence that Stadler placed the towel on the ground to give himself a line or did they zap him for building a stance? Either way, they have ended up looking like chumps.

This incident could have far reaching effects. For example, could wearing golf shoes with squared-off toe-caps be construed as providing a line? What about caps with squared-off peaks?

As professionals wear extremely colourful and expensive clothes, a new scenario could emerge at future televised US tournaments.

"Hey Rossie, how's he looking down there?"

"Well, he's in real bad shape. The ball's lying in thick, prickly bushes and the ground is real muddy but he might be able to get a swing to it. He's going in there... no, he's not, he's come out again and he's taking off his $500 cashmere sweater. He's going in again... no, he's coming out and removing his $150 shirt and his $1,500 crocodile shoes and his $300 slacks. He's wearing just a cap and his underpants. Now he's taken them off and gone in. The gallery are closing in for a better look. Ouch! I bet that hurt."

Welcome to nude golf, the hottest thing on the US Tour.

(1987)

BAK TO SKOOL

While golfers everywhere reel away from the rules with serious brain damage, the administrators of the game have now come up with the proverbial left hook to leave us lolling on the ropes. This latest blow is, of course, the new handicapping system about which you have heard and read so much, and more than probably do not understand. That means we're in this thing together but I may be able to throw a little light on the matter for I have just finished reading the complete and unexpurgated version of the *Standard Scratch Score and Handicapping Scheme 1983* as produced by the Council of National Golf Unions.

"Now pay attention class and turn to page one of your exercise books. Perkins, put that mashie niblick down! And Foskett, stop picking your nose with a tee peg!

"Today's subject is the new handicapping scheme for 1983... Perkins, the time for practice is after school... the time for listening is now, so listen you loathsome person.

"First of all there has been a change to the maximum handicap allowable for men. Can anyone tell me what it is? No, Perkins it is not three wives and two mistresses you foul-minded worm. The answer is 28. Got that class? The new maximum handicap allowable for men is 28. Good.

"Right, now we come to the question of Categories and the handicaps they cover. This may be old ground for some of you but it's worthing covering again. Category 4 golfers... and this includes you Perkins... are handicaps 28 to 21: Category 3 golfers are handicaps 20 to 13: Category 2 golfers are handicaps 12 to 6 and Category 1 golfers are handicaps 5 or better.

"Now the new system is quite simple really. As from January 1st next year, every golfer will start operating with two handicaps, his playing handicap and his exact handicap. These two handicaps will develop as you play in various competitions. Every time you compete in a competition... yes, Foskett, what is it?"

"Please Sir, how can you have two handicaps?"

"Good question, Foskett, and one I shall now answer. Every time you compete in a competition, your score, even if it is a no return, will be rated on a decimal point system.

"In Categories 2 to 4, if your nett score is anything above the Standard Scratch Score of the course then your handicap will go up 0.2. This will be your exact handicap although your playing handicap will remain the same until you have totted up more than 0.5 in which case your playing handicap will go up one stroke. No returns will count as being above SSS and be awarded the 0.2 penalty. Category 1 players only go up 0.1 for a score above the SSS. Any questions so far?

"Now listen carefully to this part. For each stroke below the SSS, you deduct a decimal number according to your Category. Thus for every stroke below SSS, a Category 4 player will deduct 0.4 from his exact handicap, a Category 3 player will deduct 0.3 from his exact handicap, a Category 2 player will deduct 0.2 from his exact handicap and a Category 1 player will deduct 0.1 from his exact handicap. When the total deducted reaches more than 0.5 then the new playing handicap is one stroke lower. None of this, of course, takes into account the fact that on January 1st of next year, we shall all be allocated one more stroke on our handicaps. Now, are there any questions? Yes, Mulliner, what is it?"

"Well Sir, if I grasp the jolly old scenario as you've outlined it then it means that a nine handicap Category 2 chappie can leg it round the links in four strokes under the SSS and still remain a nine handicap. What I mean, Sir, is that if the fella in question had an exact handicap of 9.4, his four under score would reduce him to 8.6 exact handicap but his playing handicap would be unaffected."

"Quite correct, Mulliner, but that is the whole object of the new system inasmuch as it means that the exceptionally good round, of which there may be only one in a single year, does not mean the player is instantly reduced and spends the remainder of the year playing off an unrealistic handicap. If your nine handicap player has another score below the SSS then his handicap would come down to eight. The system has been devised to provide a fairer reflection of every golfer's current form.

"This means that the old system of picking out the chairman of the handicapping committee at the bar and buying him a couple of large ones while regaling him with your tale of woe will have absolutely no effect, except to get the old toad blind drunk. In its place will operate a system without a soul, a cold merciless monster which will spit out handicaps at the touch of a button, I refer of course to... Perkins, where are you going? Perkins, come back here! Perkins, just what do you think you're doing?"

"I'm going to be a computer salesman, Sir."

(1983)

KEEP GOLF OUT OF THIS SNAKE–PIT

When, in 1930, Bobby Jones completed his Impregnable Quadrilateral of winning the Open and Amateur Championships on both sides of the Atlantic, he stood as the supreme example of the gentleman sportsman who played the game in its true spirit.

Four years later, Jones had created a lasting monument to the game in the form of Augusta National, which is now rightly regarded as a shrine to his achievements every time the US Masters comes around in April.

There now appears a strong likelihood that both Jones's contribution to the game and Augusta itself are going to be tainted by the grubby hands of the Olympic Games in 1996. Golf, which was last included in the Olympics in 1904 despite objections at the time from the Royal and Ancient, has been lobbying hard in recent times for re-entry to the Games.

For a sport to be accepted the International Olympic Committee insists that a request is made from a world federation or body with properly constituted rules and regulations.

Thus, in 1989 the World Golf Association was formed with the express purpose of gaining Olympic inclusion. This body was later restructured with the R & A and the USGA joining forces as the World Amateur Golf Council (WAGC).

Into this maelstrom of acronyms has now stepped the Atlanta Committee for the Olympic Games (ACOG) which announced last week that it wants golf, featuring men and women professionals, included in the 1996 jamboree. Furthermore, if golf is included it will be staged over the Augusta National course.

Frankly, the Olympic Games needs golf more than golf needs the Olympics. The Olympics stand for everything that golf doesn't.

In terms of international disharmony, the Olympics have no rival with a track record of Black Power protest, Arab terrorism, boycotts, cheating, bending the rules and drug abuse. Does golf wish to be associated with such activities when its clean-cut image stands far above any other sport?

The answer to this question has not been forthcoming from the WAGC, but Michael Bonallack, secretary of the R & A, stated that he felt golf's inclusion would do a great deal of good, while another view was expressed that the Olympics would bring golf to the developing nations with the financial benefits hopefully going down the line. Now we're getting a little warmer.

Although an Olympic golf event would carry no prize money for the professionals, the gold medal winners would benefit enormously from their endorsement contracts (Steffi Graf is reputed to have received $1 million from Adidas for winning the gold medal for tennis in the 1988 Games).

Of course, crucial to the whole exercise is just how much money will be generated through television and how much of it will filter back to the developing nations.

The IOC does have a fund for encouraging athletes from Third World countries, but the IOC also has a lavish headquarters and a Committee which enjoys a lifestyle of quite uninhibited extravagance. Will golf's money ever reach these developing nations, many of which are too embroiled in their own civil problems to encourage the growth of golf?

There are far too many unanswered questions for golf to go rushing into this particular snake-pit. The game has its own long-established traditions: the four major championships act as the pinnacles, the World Cup is regarded as the team championship of the professional game – an Olympic golf medal would be an irrelevance, just as it is in tennis.

This begs another question: who won the men's gold medal for tennis in this year's Olympic Games in Barcelona? I can't remember, but I do remember who won Wimbledon.

The final decision on this issue has yet to be made and the IOC may reject golf on the grounds that they are trying to cut down on the size of the Games, rather than increase them.

If they do find favour then, I'm afraid, it's move over Bobby Jones and Augusta National, your position has been usurped by the shabby commercialism of a total dishonoured movement.

(1992)

OVERCOMING HANDICAPS

A few years ago, the PGA European Tour conducted a survey in which the professionals were handicapped over a number of rounds on the same basis as club golfers.

Severiano Ballesteros emerged as the best player with a handicap of plus four while several others were plus three. Thus, whenever Ballesteros took more than 68 strokes on a par 72 course his handicap would have been adjusted upwards.

For Ballesteros to have a handicap of plus four is not perhaps that remarkable. For an amateur, to be playing off that handicap is something special; and yet at the recent Amateur Championship there was a glut of plus handicap players, including one who played off plus five.

These figures were not lost on Michael Bonallack, the Secretary of the R & A, a man who won five amateur titles but never had a handicap lower than plus two. Bonallack felt that the present handicap system allowed good players to protect their handicap too much, thereby giving them instant access to all the big amateur events without the threat of being balloted out.

His concern was that these players were not notifying their clubs of poor rounds away from home and clinging to a handicap established chiefly on their home ground.

The Council of National Golf Unions has informed us that the handicapping system foisted upon us in 1983 was designed to provide a fair reflection of a player's current ability. In reality it is a cheat's charter. It legitimises a golfer's intent to maintain a handicap at a false level, be it high or low.

Fortunately most golfers play the game in the true spirit of trying to reduce their handicap every time they play a competitive round. But the system even takes the enjoyment out of that.

"Performance anxiety" is an expression which modern psychiatrists are fond of using when discussing man's inadequacies in the area euphemistically described as "having fun with your clothes off". The same expression can now be applied to man's attempts to play the game described as "the most fun you can have with your clothes on".

Pre-1983 it didn't really matter if we played badly in a competition and, armed with this carefree attitude, it was surprising the number of times we actually played well. Now, the only carefree spirits around the clubs are those people who don't play in competition. Those of us who do twitch around on the putting green, a haunted look on our faces as performance anxiety takes its depressing hold.

A man's handicap is one of his most cherished possessions and should not be subjected to constant changes and adjustments. It is another social plus or minus.

In certain circles, the maintenance of a lowish handicap is vital if a chap wants to "get on". For example, I know of one captain of industry who rose to dizzy heights as chairman of a quango, eventually receiving a knighthood, but who was quite incapable of playing below a handicap of 26. Carrying such a burden, it came as no surprise that he eventually resigned and retired quietly to the coast.

Handicaps are, in truth, really a kind of caste system; another way of getting people to know their place. Single figure men favour playing with other single figure men, middle handicappers with middle handicappers and so on. No system is ever going to alter that.

The time has come for the Council of National Golf Unions to admit that the handicapping system needs overhauling. The fun needs to be put back into golf and performance anxiety eliminated.
(1991)

EC SHOULD GO UP IN SMOKE

Considering the amount of income that smokers provide for the Exchequer, it has always struck me as hypocritical of the Government to persist in hounding those who contribute so generously to the nation's coffers.

Now another threat is looming on the horizon in the form of the European Commission proposal to ban all tobacco advertising which, in turn, will create repercussions in sport sponsorship by tobacco companies, worth some £5 million a year in the UK. This proposal smacks of hypocrisy of the highest order since the EC spend £650 million annually subsidising tobacco farmers.

A ban on tobacco advertising would have far-reaching effects across a broad spectrum of sport for it would also extend to the promotion of sports events, banners and clothing.

Motor racing would be the hardest hit as cars are decorated to resemble 200 mph cigarette packets, but other sports such as cricket, rugby league, equestrianism and golf would also suffer.

There are three main tobacco-sponsored tournaments on the European Tour: Benson and Hedges, Dunhill and Carrolls, which between them offer £1.5 million in prize-money with an equivalent amount spent on promotion. The loss of these events would not be a crippling blow to professional golf but it would be a substantial one.

Current attitudes towards smoking place the habit somewhere between mugging old ladies and keeping a pit bull terrier; in other words, extremely anti-social.

Nowadays, it is very difficult to find a place to light up outside the privacy of your own home. Restaurants, cinemas and tube trains are no-go areas to smokers while recent surveys on "passive" smoking provide harassed executives no relief at work.

A golf course is one of the few places where the smoker can light up with impunity. There the smoking golfer can be assured that the smoke will not cause offence while, at the same time, calm any jangling nerves.

Anyone who has smoked will know the soothing effects of a cigarette at a crucial stage and of all the games that men and women play, golf is most suited to smoking before, during and afterwards.

The most famous golfer to battle with the insidious weed was Arnold Palmer. Back in the early 1960s when he was winning everything, Palmer was the archetypal smoking sportsman. Taking in a deep drag, Palmer would then throw down his cigarette, hitch up his trousers and strike the ball straight at the flag.

He exemplified everything that was macho about smoking and was the subject of a number of advertisements by a leading American tobacco company. Palmer, however, suffered from a sinus condition and was advised by his doctor to give up smoking.

In early 1964 he decided to kick the habit and promptly won the Masters by six strokes, following that with another victory shortly afterwards. Thereafter, it was all downhill for Palmer as he began to put on weight, became edgy on the course and started to miss short putts.

At the end of the year, he came over to England for the first World Match-Play Championship, backed by the Piccadilly brand name, sampled a few of the sponsors' products and won the tournament. By the following year he was a full-time smoker again.

Jack Nicklaus enjoys an occasional cigarette but never smokes on the course. Long ago he saw a television replay of one of his victories which showed him smoking and decided it set a poor example.

Nicklaus does not look a practised smoker, holding the cigarette in a rather effete manner and hardly inhaling. Ian Woosnam and Sam Torrance are hardened smokers who can be seen wreathed in smoke while on the course. Woosnam sticks with filter-tips while Torrance is a roll-your-own man.

It is noticeable that the cameras never linger on a player who is smoking during a round. This is part of the policy of not condoning "huff and puff" which applies in all sports.

This is fair enough, but as for the bureaucrats in Brussels issuing edicts concerning tobacco sponsorship, I have one suggestion as to what to do with their proposal: anyone got a match?
(1991)

Rake's Progress

The 13th hole at my home club is a fairly straightforward par four measuring around 360 yards.

Harry Colt, the architect who designed it and the other 17 holes, certainly knew his business and, with judicious use of a couple of fairway bunkers on the left, gave the player the choice of aiming to hit the ball over these obstacles from the tee or aiming away from them.

Where Colt may have gone a little over the top was in his bunkering near the green. There are four bunkers strung across the fairway, with two more located one on each side of the green.

Since the second shot, following a reasonable drive, requires no more than a 6- or 7-iron, such excessive bunkering may seem out of place. However, when the course was laid out 75 years ago the rubber-cored ball was still in its infancy in terms of technological development. The second shot must once have presented a formidable proposition, particularly when hitting into the wind.

It so happens that a few weeks ago I played in a shotgun start competition and found myself commencing operations bright and early on the 13th. Knowing my limitations from the tee, especially with the first shot of the day, I drove safely to the right half of the fairway. On viewing my second shot I had to reassure myself that I was actually on a golf course.

There, standing like sentinels by each of the five greenside bunkers, were six-feet tall, white plastic rakes, which made the route for the approach shot appear like something a skier might face on the giant slalom.

This scenario instantly raised the question as to where bunker rakes should be located. In my opinion, manufacturing rakes with a spike at one end so they can be stuck back in the ground like a spear is, if you'll forgive the pun, a pointless exercise.

There is enough potential for bad luck lurking on a golf course without inviting even more of it in the shape of a ball hitting the perpendicular rake and being deflected.

It would appear that there are two factions in the great bunker rake debate currently raging throughout the golf clubs of our land.

There are those members who insist that rakes should be left outside bunkers, either standing up or lying down, while the other viewpoint maintains that rakes should always be left in the bunker itself. The recommendation from the English Golf Union, and I emphasise it is only a recommendation, is that rakes should be left *in* the bunkers. The reasoning behind this is that a ball heading for the sand is far less likely to be deflected by a rake in the hazard than by one lying outside. Furthermore, if the rake is in the bunker it acts as a timely reminder to repair footprints.

There was a time, not so long ago, when it was rare to find a rake anywhere near a bunker. Consequently visits to the sand were a lottery dependent on whether your predecessor had effected any repairs or not. The rake's progress in recent years has certainly assisted in educating any bunker buffalos to repair their footmarks.

Putting a rake in every bunker on the course is the only way to ensure that players use them. But this can be an expensive exercise since many of them disappear in the hands of vandals.

I have noticed that some of these modern rakes carry advertising messages. One I came across recently actually said: "The sand in this bunker was supplied by Brown's Sand and Ballast", which I found a little galling. Surely it would not be too difficult to include something along the lines of "This rake has been removed from such-and-such golf club", to discourage theft.

Good manners on the golf course should include replacing divots, repairing pitch marks and always leaving a bunker in a better condition than you found it, preferably with the rake left in the sand.

One other area of etiquette which needs clarifying is who should put the flagstick back after holing out is completed? I have always believed that the first person to hole out should put the flag back, but I overheard a conversation the other day which made me think that this may not always apply.

One player asked another how he had got on in a match and received this reply: "I lost three and two but I was 14 up in putting the flag back."
(1991)

TIME TO END THE TYRANNY

Old Man Par is by a long way the most tyrannical figure in golf. This flinty-faced accountant of the game is a hard man who has no room for sentiment, never considers mitigating circumstances and is only interested in the bottom line.

This inhumanitarian approach to a game which is supposed to give pleasure has not, unfortunately, resulted in Par being rejected for the soulless creature he is. Instead he remains inviolate, impervious to the anguished cries of agony from those golfers who have failed to defeat him and providing no trace of approval for those who succeed in giving him a metaphoric poke in the eye with a sharp stick.

For most of us who have sliced, hooked, topped and shanked our way round numerous courses, Par is a remote figure. Nonetheless, he is intensely irritating as he sits there with his blasted numbers emblazoned on every tee mark, telling us what to do on each hole.

Par is, of course, the perpetrator of a gigantic confidence trick. As his figures mock us on every hole, we are lured into the mistake of trying to achieve them with, more often than not, disastrous results.

When you come to a hole which measures 465 yards you know that Par requires you to hole out in four strokes. Since two of these strokes are supposed to be with the putter, then most of that 465 yards has to be covered in two other shots.

The fact that the hole may be playing directly into the wind, is slightly uphill and the green is on a plateau, does not enter your thinking. The hole is a par four and therefore must be played in two full shots and two putts. When this fails to happen you feel inadequate, rejected and bitter.

Being a child of the Par generation, I've been feeling inadequate, rejected and bitter most of my golfing life, but that was before I discovered the true path. It was not a discovery of the Road to Damascus variety because it didn't occur until we had played nine holes.

Let me explain. We were having a game at Royal St George's and for once the sun was glinting off the waters of Pegwell Bay and the dew lay glistening on the fairway.

The competition was a Stableford and I reached the turn having barely troubled the scorer. On checking our cards at the halfway stage, my partner and I gradually realised that we had been depriving ourselves. There on the cards was not shown the cold and unrelenting Par, but the far more comfortable and friendly Bogey. Instantly the points total for the outward half was improved and the inward half became a joyous experience.

It mattered not that by now the wind was freshening and the 438 yard 13th into the corner by Prince's was out of range in two shots: it was a bogey five and we were receiving a stroke. The same applied to the 15th, 17th and 18th. Unfettered by the restrictions of Par, the game became a pleasure. Knowing that you weren't meant to reach some of the holes in two shots released the feelings of inadequacy to the extent that you suddenly found you were reaching them or getting very close.

Par and his even more unpleasant relation Standard Scratch have been foisted upon us as the standard we must meet. For the majority it is a standard we cannot maintain. I have no objection to the professionals playing to Par as it matters not how long or difficult a course is, it is merely the man with the lowest score at the end who wins. For most of us it is ludicrous to strive to reach a 474 yard hole in two shots, but knowing that we are supposed to do just that usually results in us reaching it in four shots with our tempers in tatters.

Par should be kicked out of the game along with his peculiar aviary of feathered friends we call birdies, eagles and albatrosses. Yes, I would certainly like to shoot Par – but right between the eyes.
(1983)

WRITTEN IN THE SAND

In much the same way that policemen appear to be getting younger, the onset of advancing years is indicated by one's reaction to what is generally known as "falling standards". In golf, one standard in particular has fallen and is heavily mourned.

I am not prone to losing my temper on the golf course. With the passing of the years, maturity and rheumatism in the right shoulder have rendered my club-throwing exercises futile.

But like all quiet men I can be pushed beyond the limits. I refer to the custom at most clubs, prior to competition, for the greenkeeping staff to lovingly prepare the surfaces of each bunker into a state that would not shame a Japanese sand-garden artist. With fond strokes they caress the sand, weaving intricate patterns with the rake and making it seem almost a crime to sully their handiwork.

Knowing that the bunkers are likely to be visited on at least one occasion, a handy little rake is usually left adjacent to the bunker. After all that time and effort one would think that the players would (a) smooth out any marks they made in the bunkers and (b) use the rake for doing so.

This is not always the case. Those rakes that are still left by the bunkers (the others having suffered a high mortality rate, particularly in the autumn when the leaves need clearing in the garden) rust and erode in the changing seasons. The handle becomes a breeding ground for woodworm while the metal takes on the guise of an ancient ploughshare.

Even though the rakes are not used, it is still possible for the straying golfer to effect reasonable repair on the sand. Again, I am saddened to report this is not always the case. Many of the bunkers I visit resemble the Giant's Causeway. Great craters abound, particularly in the bank where the sand vandals have stepped down into the bunker and then clambered out again by the same route.

These bunker buffalos paw the sand before making their stroke, digging deep with their hooves in what they imagine is a reasonable impression of Gary Player. Having dug right in, they then pop the ball forward on to another spot in the bunker and repeat the same destructive process.

Invariably when my ball unluckily finds a bunker it finishes in an excavation that would inspire the enthusiasm of any budding archaeologist. From this position it is virtually impossible for me to hit the ball and that's when the red mists well up and I have to be led away. Having said that, it may well be that you subscribe to the Peter Thomson rule of golf. Thomson always maintained that you tee the ball up and do not touch it again until you lift it out of the hole.

In these days, when free drops abound, that is an admirable proposal but Thomson has an addendum to his rule of golf. He also maintains that bunkers should be left alone and be allowed to develop into a wilderness of scrub and sand from which recovery would be a torturous affair.

If bunkers were left to return to their natural state then not only would that cringing fear develop into open terror but play would be slowed even further by our nomadic wanderings through the deserts of our punishment.

I accept bunkers as part of the game but I do not accept them left like a child's sandpit. Since no rule of golf can be applied to make offenders change their ways then a local rule should be enforced.

I suggest that any golfer who offends in this manner should be required to carry a rake in the bag whenever he goes out to play, and his colleagues should see that he rakes not only his footprints but theirs as well. A little community service of that nature would make sure that particular rake's progress would be a worthwhile one.

(1986)

A Metre Too Far

When we found ourselves playing away to the French throughout history, at places like Agincourt for instance, little did we realise that one day they would finally get their own back.

I refer, of course, to the great metrication campaign to make us buy our apples in kilos, our petrol in litres and our carpets in metres.

However, those nice people on the other side of the Channel have generously allowed us to keep miles and pints and, if Mrs Thatcher has her way, the pound sterling will remain sECUre.

Nevertheless, the rot has set in; and it is striking deep at the very heart of British golf as we know it. Even if our own golf might be a good five-mile (sorry, eight kilometres) walk spoiled, we know that at the end there will be a refreshing pint (0.47 litres) behind the bar.

What concerns me is whether we are going to keep the other imperial measurements, such as yards and feet and gills and drams. These are also an integral part of the game and, while the latter measurements will provide no problems for the Scots (they order their whisky in pints anyway) the rest of us, when ordering a millilitre of scotch, will have no idea how much will be lining the bottom of the glass.

On the golf course, metrication has taken over. Throughout Britain golf clubs have produced cards of the course showing the length of holes in both yards and metres, while out on the course tee-marker signs carry the same duplicated information.

Measuring in metres instead of yards means that the final figure is lower. Thus a tough par four of 437 yards becomes a moderate par-four of 400 metres. At least, that is how it will appear to every golfer educated in imperial measures.

The business of converting metres back into yards will not take place in the mind of a golfer concentrating on the lateral hip shift. And why should it?

Think also of the changes to the language of the game. When we hear of a professional missing a putt of three feet on the last green to break the course record, we can relate to the picture of anguish such a miss would induce.

If, on the other hand, we hear that the same professional missed a putt of 0.914 metres then the picture is not so clear. "Missing from 0.914 metres," we shall say scornfully. "Even I could knock it in from there."

Similarly, should we hear of a player holing a huge 15.24 metre putt on the 15th to take the lead we should probably be wondering what's so huge about 15.24 metres: not realising, unless we are in possession of a slide rule, logarithm tables and a pocket calculator, that it represents all of 50 feet.

Tales of legendary long hitting will also have their impact diminished.

The man who walks into the clubhouse and remarks that he was up at the 472-yard 5th with a drive and 7-iron is probably to be avoided, but at least one can envisage the distance and assume he is a reasonably long hitter.

The man who walks in and says he hit the 432-metre 5th with two similar shots, while also to be avoided, is likely to be met with an indifferent "so what?" Pity, too, the poor caddies faced with pacing off the course for their masters. "Hold on a minute, guv," says the caddie, fiddling with the Tour-approved logarithm tables and scratching his head. "I make it you've got 91.44 metres to the front of the green, 95.098 to the middle and 100.584 to the back."

So I put it to you. Do you know anybody who can hit a shot to 91.44 metres? On the other hand, I bet you know a few who could hit it to 100 yards.

Therefore, I make a plea to all golfers in the British Isles to join together and fight the metrication of golf. Remember that metric measurements have far-reaching effects in all walks of life – the 36-24-36 vital statistics, so dear to all men's hearts, become, in centimetres, 95-60-95, producing visions of the Press sisters.

Anyway, I've always done my measuring in golf terms. Only the other day a motorist stopped me in the village and asked me how far it was to the nearest garage. "Slight dog-leg right, two woods and a pitch," I replied.

At the hairdresser recently I asked him to lower the blades an eighth of an inch, and when one of my children inquired as to the height of the Post Office Tower I was able to inform her that it was 50 Nick Faldos, topped off with an Ian Woosnam.

(1990)

Theory and Practice

If God, as we are led to believe, made us in His image then He failed to realise that one day we might choose to pick up a stick and take a swipe at a pebble.

This lack of foresight led Him to equip us with legs and arms of equal proportions, a pair of centralised eyes, torso with an equal number of limbs and a collection of joints and muscles which allow us to bend, twist and turn in all manner of directions.

While this combination makes for symmetry and allows us to perform ordinary tasks such as climbing Mount Everest, jumping a five-bar gate or simply unscrewing the cap of the gin bottle, when it comes to the business of hitting the pebble with the stick it is utterly useless.

Doubtless the first man or woman to hit a pebble with a stick did so without thinking how it was done, but after a while, he or she would begin to wonder why the pebble could not be hit straighter and further. Other hitters would gather round and exchange views and in between inventing the wheel and discovering fire, would draw various conclusions as to what movement would make for straight and powerful hitting of the pebble. It would be at this juncture that the pebble hitters would get the first inkling that their physiology was ill-designed for their requirements.

Today's golfer, the modern equivalent of those ancient pebble hitters, faces much the same problem. God has persisted with His design and we find ourselves embarking on the job of hitting a golf ball still stuck with those symmetrical arms, legs, eyes, muscles and joints. Thus equipped, we find that to make an efficient pass at the ball we have to make one arm longer than the other, one leg shorter than the other, stiffen the joints in one arm, concave our chests and from the tip of this contorted structure peer at the ball through one eye like a Cyclops.

All of which brings me to Severiano Ballesteros. The current Open champion, seen on the face of it, is a perfectly structured human with an ability to overcome the sundry contortions golfers have to make and hit the ball with a freedom which leaves the watcher open-mouthed in wonderment.

But now I can reveal to you the secret of Ballesteros' amazing success. While dining with him recently, the talk inevitably came round to the theories surrounding the hitting of a golf ball. "How," I asked, "do you manage to hit the ball so far?" That question may seem trite since Ballesteros is built like a Pamplona bull, but many bigger men still trail the young Spaniard in length from the tee. Ballesteros said nothing in reply but simply stood up and asked me to study the length of his arms.

Suddenly, as he stood there, all was revealed. With his shoulders perfectly level, Ballesteros' right arm was almost two inches longer than his left. The discovery of this physical phenomenon allowed everything to fall into place. While you and I when addressing the golf ball have to drop our right shoulder to place the right hand in the correct position on the grip and also check that, in so doing, we have not pointed our shoulders left of the target, Ballesteros can get into the correct address position by virtue of a natural defect.

Come to think of it, just a hint of natural deformity may be the difference between being a good golfer and a champion. History can provide us with some excellent examples, not least Ben Hogan. Hogan was, in his prime, regarded as the nearest thing to perfection in the art of striking a golf ball as is humanly possible, or put another way, in the words of Gene Sarazen, "nobody covered the flag like Hogan." What may have given Hogan the edge over his contemporaries is the fact that he is naturally left-handed but chose to play golf right-handed.

Johnny Miller is another who plays right-handed while being naturally left-handed and, although his star has long since descended from the heights of 1973 to 1976, during that period he produced a brand of golf that bordered on the fantastic. Could it also not be that Ed Furgol won the 1954 US Open because of his withered left arm, rather than in spite of it?

Furgol's was not a natural defect but the result of a childhood accident after which the arm was badly set and impaired. Although his left arm was too short and the muscles atrophied it was permanently locked, thereby allowing him to overcome a fault which plagues thousands of golfers.

Consider, too, the case of Vicente Fernandez, the current PGA champion. He won that title at St Andrews in May playing through some of the vilest weather imaginable. But Fernandez had one priceless advantage over his rivals – he was playing every stroke from a slight uphill lie simply because he was born with his right leg shorter than his left. Most golfers when playing from a slight uphill line find themselves hitting a better shot than normal.

Indeed Douglas Bader, who lost both legs in a pre-war flying accident, discovered the same. He could ensure permanent uphill stance for every shot by simply sawing an inch or two from his right leg.

The real clincher to my theory, however, is none other than Jack Nicklaus. His edge over his rivals is not provided by any apparent physical oddities but via more subtle route – Nicklaus is colour blind. This may strike one as being a disadvantage until one considers that at most tournaments nowadays the leader-boards show a player's figures, in relation to under-par scores, in red.

To Nicklaus these figures appear black, thereby providing him with the mental confirmation that he is far ahead of any other player in the field.

If God wants to produce the ideal golfer then He should create a being with a set of unequal arms and likewise legs, an elbow-free left arm, knees which hinge sideways and a ribless torso from which emerges, at an angle of 45 degrees, a stretched neck fitted with one colour-blind eye stuck firmly on the left side. And please God, let him be British.
(1979)

ON AND OFF DAYS

It has always struck me that golf must be the most perverse of all games simply because there are so many things that can go wrong. There is such a fine line between excellence and abomination that it is a wonder we get any of the components working at all.

This was brought home to me recently by Nick Faldo who, reflecting on what for him has been a mediocre year, commented: "Something has always been a little off."

Being "off" is, of course, relative. For Faldo it has been his touch on and around the greens, which I am convinced, although I haven't told him so yet, is a result of his adding more muscle last winter.

For the majority of us, being "off" covers a much broader area. There's driving, fairway woods and long irons, middle and short irons, chipping and pitching and, finally, putting. Usually one or more of these departments is "off" and the trick is to ascertain which are the most important ones to keep "on".

I have always maintained that anyone who could drive the ball straight for about 220 yards and hole everything under six feet could play comfortably to scratch.

This places driving and putting in the top categories. But, and this is where the perversity comes in, how often do we find that the driving has deserted us while the putter suddenly becomes red hot? Conversely, there are days when the tee shots soar away down the middle but we putt, as P G Wodehouse once described it, "like a sheep with the botts".

How then do we get all the departments working at maximum efficiency at the same time? If I knew the answer to that I would have retired many years ago having sold the secret for a handsome figure. Other than hard work and practice on a professional scale, there is no easy route to this ideal.

Yet, such are the strange workings of the human psyche that there can be days when you simply cannot put a foot wrong. Every shot is out of the middle of the club, every iron is crisply struck, pitch shots squirm to a halt by the flag and the hole is as big as a bucket. This state of grace cannot be acquired or conjured up – it just happens for no apparent reason.

Professionals call this "being in the zone" and that's when they come close to breaking 60. For the rest of us being in the zone can mean breaking 90 for the first time, or 80 or 70. You may be interested to know that it has happened to me, and if you've got a couple of hours, I'll tell you about it.

For the sake of brevity, all I will say here is that it was the most extraordinary experience in that I felt I could make the golf ball do anything. It wouldn't have mattered if I'd lined up facing midwicket or extra cover, I would still have delivered the ball straight down the fairway. Faced with a shot to the flag, I just nailed the ball straight at it. If I did miss a green the approach finished stone dead and I couldn't miss from ten feet. It all added up to five birdies and two eagles, marred only by a six at the short 16th when I awoke from my trance and realised the enormity of what I was doing.

Naturally, I couldn't wait to play again, believing that at last I had cracked it. But, of course, I hadn't. The magic had gone and although it returned on a few more occasions, advancing years coupled with fading powers of concentration and a feckless putter have rendered it just a pleasant memory. Nonetheless, I am grateful it happened at all for it is rare to strike one vintage shot in a round let alone a series of them.

Most of us are content with that singular moment of perfection, the unexpected melding of muscle and sinew which contrives to deliver the clubhead at exactly the right angle and direction and produce a shot of staggering virtuosity.

This is what brings us back the next time, but it is also part of golf's great delusion, the ability it has to lure us into believing that the one perfect shot is our normal game.

This is exemplified by the old story of the man sitting disconsolately in the locker room after a really "off" day. "I just didn't play my normal game," he lamented, then added: "Come to think of it, I *never* play my normal game." (1991)

TIGERS FROM THE TEE

Of all the strokes in golf there is one which encapsulates the entire appeal of the game. While the successful execution of a delicate chip shot or the holing of a long putt may provide the pleasure of having put one over the implacable enemy of par, nothing compares with the feeling of a sumptuously struck drive which soars off into the blue and bounds down the middle of the fairway.

Any golfer who has accomplished this sees no reason why it cannot be repeated from the next tee, but lightning rarely strikes twice and the ensuing heave and lunge generally disappoints.

Hitting the ball consistently a long way off the tee has always held a special fascination and exponents of the art can command a large following. Thus do the siege-gun drives of Greg Norman draw gasps from the crowd in much the same way as those of Jack Nicklaus did in the early Sixties and, going much further back, those of Ted Ray, the 1912 Open champion who, when asked how the ball could be hit further, replied: "Hit a bloody sight harder, mate."

Of course, long hitting alone does not a champion make and many players had their fame founded on muscle rather than the ability to produce low scores.

Chief among these was George Bayer, a giant American who played the tour for about 12 years from 1955. Bayer won four tournaments, including the 1957 Canadian Open, but it was his tee shots which earned him his place in the record books.

Standing 6ft 5ins and weighing 250lbs, Bayer's longest measured drive was one of 420 yards, struck during the 1953 Las Vegas Invitational. It was measured as a precaution against litigation since the ball struck a spectator who, understandably, was ill-prepared for such an occurrence. Bayer was reputed to have driven within chipping distance of a 589-yard hole, a blow which travelled over 500 yards aided apparently by a strong following wind and bone-hard ground.

The reason such titans of the tee enjoy limited success is simply geometric. Basically, as the distance increases the angle of safety narrows – an error of one degree at impact might leave us ten yards off the fairway. For someone like Bayer the ball will travel on the incorrect line much further, resulting in anything up to a 50-yard deviation.

This was clearly demonstrated to me recently when I attended a golf clinic given by a certain Evan Williams. The venue was the Belmont Hotel and Golf Club in Bermuda, a place to be recommended during a British February, and Williams had been flown in to flex his muscles in front of some visiting tourists.

For those of you who may not have heard of Williams, nick-named "Big Cat", he is a former long-driving champion of America, one of his victory drives measuring 353 yards, and he now earns his living by giving exhibitions of his power.

"Big Cat" opened his act by hitting a few 160-yard wedge shots, most of which stayed on the fairway. He then progressed through the irons, ending with a 4-iron which he struck about 240 yards. At this stage fewer balls were remaining in play and when he moved to the driver it became evident why he keeps away from tournament golf.

The ball was launched well over 300 yards with each shot but the distances of landing between one that was hooked and one that was blocked to the right would have put Williams on another golf course, or possibly, in the case of Bermuda, lost at sea.

Looking at Williams' 6ft 5in, 15-stone frame, it is easy to see why he is a tiger from the tee while the rest of us are mere tabbies. His *pièce de resistance* was to drive the ball through 300 pages of the Bermudian telephone directory, the ball continuing on another 50 yards afterwards.

I cannot resist mentioning that he was unable to obtain long distance from this particular shot.
(1990)

SHARP PRACTICE

The day when, as the inimitable P G Wodehouse so aptly put it: "All Nature cried 'Fore!'", has undoubtedly arrived.

Although you may be reading this as heavy rains sweep across the country just in time for the Bank Holiday, the recent spell of fine weather must have stirred the senses of golfers everywhere and filled them with that irresistible urge to get out on the course.

But how many of them, I wonder, would have arrived on the 1st tee and, with creaking joints and muscles, expected to drive the ball far and true down the fairway? The answer is practically all of them and, similarly, practically all of them were doomed to disappointment.

The idea of loosening up prior to a round by hitting a few shots is still alien to the British way of golf. Even if a course does possess a practice ground, it is under-used and on courses with a lengthy history, the practice ground is quite likely to be part of one of the existing holes. This is a throw-back to the days when to practise before a round was considered tantamount to cheating and not quite the done thing, particularly among gentlemen; therefore, no practice ground was created. Those days are now past and practising is acceptable for those players who wish to avail themselves of it.

However, it is one thing to practise and it is entirely another to practise usefully. Most of us, when we practise, have very little idea what indeed we are practising.

We are exhorted by the top professionals to practise assiduously in order to groom our swings and create muscle memory for when we are on the course. What we end up doing is grooming our swing faults and committing them to memory.

For example, there is a player at my club who must have been divorced long ago, such is his devotion to the practice ground. He is out there in all weathers, all the year long, pounding balls, all of which curve in that sickeningly familiar left-to-right slicing arc.

I watched him drive off the 1st tee the other day and, as his ball winged its way toward the right-hand rough, I heard him mutter: "Damn it, I've been practising all week to get rid of that slice." The point was that his swing fault was so ingrained there was nothing he could do about it.

One of the amazing things about practising is that if you are hitting, say, a 5-iron, you will find that, out of 30 or so balls, half-a-dozen will be complete fluffs, while the majority of the remainder will be grouped roughly in a reasonably tight area. Yet there will always be one which is 15 yards further on than all the rest. And it is quite likely that this particular ball is the oldest and scruffiest in the bag. The point is that because of its shabby state, you swing at it without expecting any startling results. It flew painlessly away and there it is, luring you into thinking you can hit all your 5-iron shots that far.

The chief drawback about practising is having to find the balls afterwards. If you are an erratic striker, this means you are trudging hither and thither and as you pick them up, you finally have to face up to one of the game's immutable laws; namely the number of balls retrieved is always fewer than the number hit.

To avoid this, you can of course visit a driving range, but the balls supplied here not only have the compression of a rice pudding but also exhibit the flight characteristics of a wounded grouse.

The ideal practice conditions are those found at professional tournaments. For a start, your caddie carries your clubs there, an unlimited supply of balata-covered balls awaits your pleasure and, should something go wrong, there are several gurus prowling up and down to put you right.

With such facilities available, it is not surprising these people improve while the rest of us struggle. Practising under the eye of a professional is probably the best way to improve, provided the lines of communication are clearly established.

I remember one lesson I had from a rather over-zealous professional in which he walked 100 yards up the practice area, stuck a shooting stick in the ground and asked me to try and hit it. My first shot struck the shooting stick and the next shot knocked it over. "Right," said the professional, "now I'll tell you what you are doing wrong."
(1991)

SWINGING TOWARDS CHAOS THEORY

Golfers are being continually bombarded with new theories and methods. We live in an age of programmed swings. The era of the natural player is past, lost in a welter of regimented uniformity.

The question is: when will it all end? The answer: never. As long as golfers seek the Holy Grail of perfection, they will continue to analyse, consult and alter their methods.

Golfers are constantly exposed to science; it lurks in books, articles, videos and on the course. Now that Fred Couples and John Daly are the two hottest items in the game, it is only a matter of time before several books explaining the secrets of their success hit the market.

Thousands of golfers will devour their recommendations and try to emulate their techniques. What we fail to realise is that these players are immensely powerful, and can probably ensure the wind is behind them just by blowing their noses. Despite these differences, we follow their advice with disastrous and painful results.

Scientific theory really hurts on the course. We can go out in the morning of a 36-hole competition and record a reasonable score, but we are not happy.

As we sit over our treacle tart and Kummel at lunchtime, we reflect on our rounds and work out where we could have saved shots.

We deduce that we were not hitting our drives far enough, so all we have to do is make a slight adjustment to our swings, as recommended by Fred and John, and we will knock at least six strokes off our score.

When we start our afternoon round, however, we find things are not going as expected, and we change another part of the swing. So it goes on, until we are found somewhere in the vicinity of the 14th green, making an early declaration of our innings.

This is a classic case of too much theory, even down to the treacle tart and Kummel, which, theorists would have us believe, assist with the putting.

I can vouch for the efficacy of Kummel as a cure for putting ills. Many years ago, in a 36-hole club match, after I had three-putted six times in the morning, my opponent for the afternoon, an older and craftier man, suggested I drank six Kummels. I do not recollect three-putting once after that, but I do not remember hitting any other shots either, since I was prostrate on the locker-room floor in a deep slumber.

Further agony is inflicted when we visit the practice ground, where, while we are trying to eradicate a duck-hook of boomerang proportions, we are approached by the club theorist. The first inkling we have of his presence is the sight of a pair of white golf shoes (specially dulled to prevent reflection from the sun), with turned-up toes (for greater leverage in the hitting area) and extra long spikes (for more height to gain a wider arc). We pretend we have not noticed the white shoes, and carry on determinedly, still hitting them quail-high in the direction of square-leg.

Then we hear: "Tut, tut, such a pity to waste what could be a sound method." We look up and reply: "What do you mean?"

"Well," says the club theorist, "it's obvious. Your weight transference is all wrong. You're swinging too much inside, letting go at the top, and not using your right hand at all."

The club theorist then moves on, leaving what little confidence we did have in tatters, happy to have scored yet another victory in the cause of science and analysis. What is needed to combat this obsession with science is a return to the natural way of doing things. Think what would happen if we analysed our eating methods – bent left arm, slow cutting action with the right hand, cock the left wrist, before placing the food in the mouth. We would probably end up feeding our ears.

This thirst for knowing how and why has got to stop. The scientists have had their way too long. Look at it this way. Did Einstein ever go round a rain-lashed Carnoustie in 71? Are the whole of the staff of NASA scratch men? There's your answer.

To illustrate how futile this theorising is, remember the golfer who used the interlocking grip to cut his wedding cake. He still only managed a slice. (1992)

BRED ANY GOOD HOOKS LATELY?

There is no doubt that instructional books and magazine articles can drastically improve your game. Only the other day I arranged two piles of magazines on the floor, positioned about the width of my shoulders apart, and with the heaviest tome from my library balanced gently on top of my head, managed to eliminate a destructive sway which had been plaguing me for months.

Most golfers make the mistake of trying to assimilate what is presented to them in these various publications with invariably disastrous results.

The old adage that a golfer can only cope with one or two swing thoughts at a time just does not apply to the really dedicated golf theorist. Having absorbed every piece of advice from Braid to Ballesteros, the dedicated theorist is still hungry for more.

He or she pounces on the latest instructional tip with all the fever of a drug addict reaching for a syringe. And, in a matter of moments, he has adopted the posture recommended and is making simulated swings with the nearest available object, such as umbrella, fountain pen, ruler, cat, etc.

The extraordinary thing about all this thirst for knowledge is that you never meet anyone who will admit to reading an instructional book or article. "Never bother with them, old boy," is the usual reaction if you mention that such-and-such a professional recommends a slight flaring of the nostrils for greater power and impact. Yet, there must be an army of secret addicts out there, men and women with huge libraries containing every word on the intricacies of the golf swing, otherwise there would not be such a plethora of golf books, magazines and videos in the market-place.

What many people do not realise is there is a world of difference between learning the game and being taught the game. Learning the game is a childhood voyage of discovery, being taught the game is brain damage for adults. When you and I were learning to construe Virgil, people like Ballesteros were learning to bend the ball round a clump of trees while standing on one leg with both eyes closed. In later life, it's professionals like him who are doing the teaching and it's us who are being taught.

It's all a conspiracy really. Before anyone becomes a professional, he or she has to take a solemn oath not to reveal the real secret of golf. This brotherhood, who shake hands with each other using the interlocking grip, know that their very livelihood depends on keeping the secret locked away from prying amateur eyes.

Some people say the secret is kept in a watertight chest at the bottom of the lake in front of the 18th at The Belfry, others believe it is concealed in a microdot on the end of Lord Derby's nose in the painting which hangs in the PGA reception area. Wherever it is, the professionals guard it with their lives.

Therefore, it was with a hollow laugh that I read that the PGA of America have produced what they consider the ultimate coaching guide. Their *PGA Teaching Manual* contains 624 pages, 20 chapters, more than 400 photographs and took more than five years to complete. Designed primarily for professionals, the manual is also available to the general public and will doubtless sell in its thousands.

Another guaranteed best seller is *The Golf Swing* by David Leadbetter (Collins Willow, £12.95), currently the hottest guru in golf. Billed as the most revolutionary instruction book since Ben Hogan's *Modern Fundamentals*, this book's main premise is the mastering of the athletic golf swing.

Much of its contents make very good sense if you happen to be 6ft 3in tall, weigh 14 stone and have worked exclusively on its method for five years. If your name isn't Nick Faldo however, then hang on to the day job.

To my mind, all this information on the swing can only create confusion. Look out for Sandy Lyle. There he was, ambling amiably along with his mind free of any technical thoughts, winning plenty of tournaments plus the odd major championship. Now he's trussed up like a chicken in harnesses while everyone wants to give him advice. If ever there is a case of paralysis through analysis it is Lyle.

The answer lies in keeping the brain totally inactive. If a frontal lobotomy is too drastic a measure, try thinking of something really boring – like the square grooves issue, one of Jimmy Tarbuck's jokes, or possibly the other 16 holes at The Belfry. Pretty soon you'll find your brain is completely empty and you will be free to concentrate solely on playing what I call "Mindless Golf". Come to think of it, that's not a bad title. What's more, there might even be a book in it.

(1990)

EXORCISING GLADYS

The trouble with New Year resolutions is they always involve giving up something you enjoy, causing a pang of conscience the first time you rummage desperately for a cigarette or reach furtively for the gin bottle.

Having been brought up to resist anything except temptation, the resolutions business leaves me relatively unmoved, but it could serve some useful purpose if we could resolve to give up something we palpably don't enjoy.

Obviously things like paying income tax or having a tooth out are beyond the scope of my suggestion, but when applied to golf a whole new realm of possibilities becomes apparent.

After a lifetime's love-hate relationship with the game I have reached the the conclusion that golf has passed me by. There was a time back in the mid-1960s when I could play a bit. I remember once being all square with two to play in a match and taking a 3-iron for my second to the long 17th and just drilling it in there and... well, I won't go on because the thing about people talking about their own game is that it prevents you talking about yours.

The legacy of the 1970s is a shot which, 20 years later, is still with me. It's a painful process even to try to describe this execrable stroke, but its chief characteristic is revealed by the ball flying feebly into the air towards extra cover, in other words, a Gladys.

I've often wondered about Gladys, who she is, where she comes from. In my imagination she is an elderly lady who displays a religious fanaticism for the game but whose stultified swing only succeeds in sending the ball pathetically into the right rough.

I've tried to exorcise Gladys by visiting various high priests of instruction, but although some have provided temporary relief Gladys has always returned with a tenacity which belies her advancing years.

Getting rid of Gladys has become an obsession; why should I have to pay golfer's alimony to this hoary old bat? But Gladys is cunning; she leaves little notes around for my brain to pick up.

I remember at one Open Championship listening to a notable player explaining that his 67 was all due to using a shorter left thumb on his grip. Minutes later another notable player came in with a 66 and he put it all down to a longer left thumb on his grip. I tried them both, neither worked and all the time Gladys was sniggering away in the background.

Worse still, I know why Gladys appears and on occasions, with a supreme mental effort, I can send her packing for maybe 17 holes. But then she suddenly pops up with her stultified swing and there I am trooping off towards the right rough again.

All of which bring me to my New Year resolution to give up something I don't enjoy. In 1993 I shall free myself of Gladys and stride out into a brave new world where all my drives will fly straight and true with just a hint of draw.

I know there's a possibility I shall be visited by Glady's stepbrother, Snap Hook, but I don't care. I can deal with him because I had him in the 1960s. If he returns then at least I shall be hitting the thing instead of patting it like a friendly puppy.

Come to think of it, it was at the end of the 1960s I decided to get rid of Snap Hook and work on a controlled fade and now here I am trying to do exactly the reverse. That's the trouble with having just a little knowledge – it can be dangerous.

There was a time, back in the 1950s, when I simply walked up to the ball and hit it. I didn't think how I was going to hit it; I just looked at the ball and the target and joined the two.

Perhaps instead of resolving to rid myself of Gladys specifically I should resolve not to theorise about golf any more. But that would take away a great deal of the enjoyment from a game which is still the most fun you can have with your clothes on.

(1993)

Box of Tricks

If, like me, you have been confined to barracks these past few weeks due to festive commitments and a sodden course, you may be interested in a little indoor training exercise.

The purveyor of this tip was John Stirling, the professional at Meon Valley, who recommends it to all his pupils. Just take your sand-wedge, hold it straight out horizontally in front of you and write your name and address in the air with the club head.

It is not as easy as it sounds. Having written my name out in full my arms were beginning to sag and I was wishing I had been christened something shorter. I struggled on through the house name, the road, the village, the town and the county (Buckinghamshire, if you please) and it took a huge mental effort to add the post code. The purpose of this exercise is to train the hands to receive the message from the brain and transfer it to the club head. This,

I have always felt, is the key to an imaginative short game: if the hands are sufficiently trained then they instinctively know what to do with the club head as it approaches the ball.

Another good exercise is bouncing a ball on the face of a wedge and seeing how many times you can keep it going. In the days of the old small Dunlop 65, with a balata cover, I could manage 50 bounces without too much trouble. With the advent of the Surlyn cover and the solid ball the thing just pings off the club face at indiscriminate height and is much harder to control. This should tell you that a solid ball is useless for little touch shots around the green.

Most of the professionals are extremely adept at bouncing the ball. I remember at the US Masters when Roberto de Vicenzo was standing by the 1st tee idly bouncing a ball on his wedge before going out for a practice round. An enthusiastic spectator asked de Vicenzo how long he could keep the ball bouncing. "As long as I want," came the reply. Whereupon a bet was struck that Vicenzo couldn't walk the length of the 1st hole at Augusta (400 yards) bouncing the ball all the way. Off he set, followed by the eager punter: occasionally he would stage a mock stumble just to keep the interest going but such was his control it was like taking candy from a baby.

At the highest level golf is all about two forms of control – ball control and self-control. Some of the most brilliant shot-makers have never won a tournament because, although they found the act of hitting balls relatively easy, they could never master the actual game of golf.

They were, however, sharp enough to turn their ability into a handsome living by becoming trick-shot specialists. The first of these was Joe Kirkwood, who emigrated to America from Australia in 1920. He became friendly with Walter Hagen and the two of them toured the country giving exhibitions.

Kirkwood developed his act into a *tour de force*. He could hit two balls simultaneously and cause them to cross in mid-flight, one slicing and the other hooking. He would bury a ball in the ground so only the top was visible and then hit it 200 yards using a 4-wood. He would tee up six balls in a line and hit them, alternately hooking and slicing.

British professional Noel Hunt now dominates the trick-shot scene. Hunt gave his all on the tournament trail but never quite hit the big time. Eventually he could take the disappointment no longer and went to work on developing a lucrative trick-shot routine. His act is well worth catching.

Another development in this area has been devised by American professional Peter Jacobsen, who has won several tournaments. Jacobsen has a talent for mimicking other players' swings and mannerisms and has created an act even the victims watch.

He can adopt the unorthodox lunge of Lee Trevino, the calculated intensity of Jack Nicklaus, the flailing finish of Arnold Palmer or the uninhibited style of Severiano Ballesteros. The only problem for Jacobsen is that he is never quite sure how to find his own swing when he goes out to play. (1991)

ON YOUR BIKE

It was a fit of middle-aged madness that started the whole thing off. A few years ago I looked in the mirror one morning and, although I knew the name, I couldn't quite place the face.

Could this be the same young blade who once played four rounds in a single day at Carnoustie and still had enough energy afterwards to dance the night away? The answer, reflected back through the red mists of an early morning coughing fit, was in the negative – it was not the same man and, with time having left its imprint, something had to be done.

Psychologists are fond of informing us that a sudden urge to get fit is very common among men of, shall we say, advancing years, so it was gratifying to know that the *mens sana in corpore sano* feeling which has swept over me was not merely an individual whim. What really presented the problem was how this state could be achieved as painlessly as possible with the minimum of effort.

The problem was not about losing weight but maintaining what little I had in an operable state. This condition first manifested itself at school where the distance I grew upwards was disproportionate to the width I grew outwards.

At school it fell upon me, because of my height, to be included in the rugby team as a lock-forward. The dreadful imbalance this created caused me to be squeezed from the scrum like toothpaste and left extruded on the playing fields purported to have acted as a training ground for the Battle of Waterloo. It came as no surprise when I was taken aside by the sports masters, who told me in a voice quivering with emotion that in future I would be "excused rugby".

Now, a few decades later, I faced the situation which, if nothing was done, could have meant being excused golf.

Then I hit upon the very thing. What I needed was a set of wheels. A few telephone calls revealed that my wishes could be fulfilled, the wheels were ordered and arrived within a few days.

The assembly instructions were quite clear and informed me that the wheels could be made functional in 30 minutes. My fitness programme actually began right then, things mechanical not being my forte, and two hours later I emerged sweating but triumphant with the wheels ready to roll.

The next problem was where to site the machine. At the time we were living in quite a small house but eventually we found a convenient spot in the bathroom, between WC and wash basin.

The first Sanitary Ware Hill Climb began the next day. Lining the shelf in front of me with postcards depicting scenic views of the French Alps, I donned shorts and a yellow jersey. I even considered, remembering that it cut down wind resistance, shaving my legs but decided against it.

I mounted the steed and set off. I didn't actually go anywhere but I made the wheels go round and in no time at all the speedometer had whipped up to 20mph. "This is the life," I said to myself, as I sped through one *arrondissement* after another, the joys of the open bathroom, the scent of deodorant in the nostrils, the fresh condensation filling the lungs.

On some of my longer runs my wife would come in and throw a bucket of water over me or bring me a soft drink in a plastic flask with a straw sticking out of the top.

I kept at it for a year during which time I racked up over 1,000 miles. Due to lack of sponsorship for the prime space on the back of the yellow jersey and a few technical problems, mostly relating to enthusiasm, I gave up.

Now the wheels reside in the boxroom, tucked away out of sight. I occasionally give them a desultory spin but the desire for an extended run has gone. One thing did emerge from all this, however. The whole exercise brought a new meaning to the expression "On yer bike".
(1983)

HORIZONTALLY CHALLENGED

I have always been deeply suspicious of golfers who claim they have never had a lesson in their lives as they are usually the very ones who would benefit from an extensive course of therapy from their club professional.

On the other hand, there are those golfers for whom lessons are their lifeblood, the fix they need before they can even contemplate swinging at a ball.

Unfortunately, I am one of these, a confirmed lesson junkie who, after the slightest miss-hit during a round can be found the following day occupying the practice ground under the sympathetic eye of the current guru.

It all started when I was about six or seven and came under the jurisdiction of a professional called Herbert Rhodes. At that age, he appeared a giant of a man, resplendent in a plus-four tweed suit and with a bucolic glow to his cheeks. He was nicknamed "Slasher" for the speed and violence of his swing, which propelled the ball vast distances but sadly, not always in the right direction.

My only memory of my time with him was when my mother came out to see how I was progressing with my lessons and, in attempting to emulate "Slasher's" power and lightning attack, I swung myself off my feet and fell flat on my face in the mud.

Metaphorically speaking, I have been falling flat on my face ever since.

During the 1950s I adopted the Cotton Brace which I picked up from studying pictures of Henry Cotton. The essence of this was to create the rigidity of a telegraph pole in the left leg and let the hands and arms swing past it.

At the time I was using a grip which could have strangled an anaconda and I do recall that off the 1st tee in one British Boys' Championship I nearly wiped out the entire Walker Cup selection committee, who were standing somewhere between square leg and mid-wicket.

The next staging post on this particular potholed road was the Palmer Crouch with Pirouette. This involved a radical restructuring of the grip whereby instead of exhibiting five knuckles on the left hand as I had previously, barely half a knuckle was in view. The knees were bent to such an extent that any straightening of them would have caused the club to pass a foot above the ball and the whole thing was finished off with the left arm extending down the line to provide that familiar whirling finish.

This one was totally hook-proof and it was also the one which went off a little early one year and rocketed into the starter's tent in the Roseberry Bowl at Ashridge.

About 15 years ago I developed the Ornithological Prod. This resulted from reading a book by Johnny Miller in which he stated that you should grip the club as though you were holding a bird.

On the occasions I imagined I was holding a wren or a linnet, when the club head reached the ball it was travelling so slowly it produced a gentle curving flight which sent the ball to earth about a hundred yards from the tee. In trying to inject a little more pace and impact I found that my grip had taken on the intensity of a man trying to hold down an Andean condor.

In more recent time I have dabbled with the Ballesteros Early Wrist Cock, which produced the one which would have gone over the starter's tent if one had been there.

There has been the Faldo Mechanical, which involves turning the shoulders to and fro in metronomic repetitiveness with hardly any arm swing and then there was the Strange Lurch, courtesy of Curtis.

The Lurch was reasonably successful for a while as it ensured a massive distribution of weight. One day, however, it all went horribly wrong. It was on the 12th at Sunningdale when I was going for a really big one round the corner to shorten the second shot.

I started off fairly slowly but by the time the club had reached hip height I had a vague inkling that things were getting out of control.

By the time the arms had reached the top, all the weight was on the right side and the ball appeared to be about six feet away.

Poised like a heron by a pool I gave the edifice one more turn and slowly toppled over to land flat on my face again. As I lay there it dawned on me that in 40 years of playing the game I had, horizontally speaking, come full circle.
(1991)

TOURNAMENT SCENE

MASTERS' BLOCK

Forget all that stuff you read about the pressure of the Masters, ignore all the comments from the players about driving down Magnolia Avenue and that special feeling it inspires, disregard the legends of Augusta – what we are facing here is a real crisis.

What we are facing is a severe case of Masters overkill. It's all right for Jack Nicklaus, Severiano Ballesteros, Nick Faldo, Ian Woosnam and Sandy Lyle, they *know* what they'll be doing round about the second week of April.

All they have to do is get themselves and their clubs to Georgia and a courtesy car will do the rest. Once they get there, they have their own locker in the clubhouse, they are waited on hand and foot by a series of flunkies and they can practise as much as they wish. With that kind of treatment it's hardly surprising they shoot 66.

What they don't have to do is sit down a week or two before the Masters and wonder what they can say about it that's fresh and interesting. They get out on the course every day and can see at first hand what changes have been made, how the sand is in the bunkers and how fast the greens are.

They can impart their feelings on these matters but there's nothing like experiencing it yourself to form a proper opinion which you can then convey to your readers.

Since there is no chance of you playing the course during Masters week your only hope is to book a tee-time on the Monday afterwards, always provided you're prepared to stand in a line of Japanese photographers.

Previewing the Masters makes competing in it seem like child's play. After all, what can you say about Nicklaus's Masters record that hasn't been said before? You could say it's awesome but using the word awesome to describe Nicklaus is now the equivalent of a full-blooded shank out of bounds.

All right you say, let's try Ballesteros, there's a lot of scope there surely? There's dashing, swashbuckling, spectacular, charismatic just for a start.

Having written the words Severiano Ballesteros more times than I've three-putted I'm hoping to give my fingers a rest. As for those other descriptions, they were long ago consigned to the attic of my brain.

Let's hear it about the course then. Give the troops some of the Bobby Jones-Alistair Mackenzie-Fruitlands Nursery-building-a-dream-course stuff. Talk about the influence of Augusta on course architecture, mention how even Nicklaus has paid tribute to the design with derivative holes at his own Muirfield Village.

Throw in some history: you know, the Gene Sarazen albatross in 1935, the Palmer charge in 1960, Peter Oosterhuis leading after three rounds in 1973, Tom Weiskopf finishing runner-up four times.

Talk about the great moments, the triumphs and disasters – Player winning in 1978, Sneed losing the following year, Crenshaw finally winning a major title in 1984 and Lyle, Faldo and Woosnam making us all proud to be British over the past four years.

I know, I know, it's all there, but you don't seem to understand. I've been doing it for over 20 years and there's not a lot left in this particular horse. We are not machines. Masters previews do not tumble from us like the cascading waters of Rae's Creek. Occasionally, the works seize up, grind to a halt and are in need of an overhaul.

So what am I going to write about in the run-up to the 1992 Masters? I haven't the faintest idea but I expect I'll think of something.
(1992)

WITH APOLOGIES TO O.B. KEELER

Hoylake 1930. It is with a sense of wonderment and awe that I deliver this dispatch concerning the crowning of the new Open Champion for never in all my years of following him has the Champion put me through such a maelstrom of conflicting emotions. What he must have suffered during that final fateful day hardly bears thinking about and that he emerged triumphant, but not, I hasten to add, unscathed is tribute more to his strength of character than the quality of his game.

Before embarking upon the main event concluded on the Wirral Peninsula, I am reminded of what the new Champion said to me after he had brought the recent British Amateur Championship to a successful conclusion. I asked him at the time if his victory would increase his determination to win the Open

Championship also. "On the contrary," he replied decisively, "I'll do what I can of course. But I can't start breaking my back over anything else for a while. I'm too happy and too thankful to have managed to win here. There could be nothing in golf today that I wanted so much. I can't believe it really happened now."

He had, during that week at St Andrews, drawn deep on his competitive fires and now he had to stoke them up again if he were to accomplish what everyone else expected of him at Hoylake.

I will not dwell on the first two days of play but instead avail you of the positions at the beginning of the last day's play when 61 golfers took the field with the Champion leading by a single stroke at 142, two strokes better than par for the great Hoylake course at full stretch. Next on 143 came Fred Robson, the leading British challenger, and he was followed by Horton Smith on 145, and Archie Compston, Mac Smith and Leo Diegel were grouped together on 147. That the morning of the last day belonged to Compston there is no doubt. Playing like a frenzied giant, this colossus of British golf gained five strokes on the Champion in the first four holes after the Champion had made as ghastly a start as is imaginable. Compston reached the turn in 34 and had made up three of his five stroke deficit as the Champion pulled himself together after the first three holes and from the 4th to the 14th was four under fours. But when Compston began his inward half with a blistering rush of 3-3-3-2, the Champion could only step with him for part of the way and Archie had caught him again. Compston finished with a 68, breaking the course record into pieces, while the Champion limped in with a 74 and thus they stood at 215 and 216 respectively.

Under a blackening sky and with a sprinkle of rain in the air, they set off in the final round. While it is impossible for one reporter to be in four places at once, I think I can tell you where Compston lost his lead; where Diegel went down and where the Champion won.

The Champion received his break at the 2nd hole when his drive flew too far to the right and then bounced off the head of steward to land in a bunker at least 30 yards off line. From the sand he played a splendid pitch to the green and sank a 20-foot putt for an improbable birdie. This acted as a spur to the Champion and he played beautifully up to the 8th. Just as I can tell you of the hole that won the Championship, so can I recall where he nearly lost it. On this hole of 482 yards, he had been reaching the green regularly with a drive and a spoon. On this occasion he hit a good drive and a good second which broke away to the left of the green down a slight slope but in no sort of trouble. It is beyond my comprehension, and it was beyond the comprehension of all who saw it, how he managed to effect five more strokes on the ball before it vanished down the hole, but effect them he did and this is how he did so. For his third shot, he elected to play a simple run-up shot. He missed the shot. That is the only explanation. The ball finished feebly short. He then decided to chip and left the ball 10 feet short and his features were suffused with anger. He naturally went for the five, missed by 12 inches, walked and hit it again without looking and there was a seven.

"It was the most inexcusable hole I ever played," he said, "An old man with a croquet mallet could have got down in two. I will play that hole over a thousand times in my dreams."

I had seen the Champion suffer nightmares before but never one like this on a simple, straightforward hole where he was pin-high in two and took a seven. Right then I began to agree with Miss Joyce Wethered that competitive golf was a game not worth the candle.

He turned in 38 and played the last nine in 37. The last five holes in one over fours was the winning streak, especially the 4-4-4 on the last three. He entered the clubhouse with a total of 291 and awaited his fate, which now lay in the hands of Diegel and Macdonald Smith. Compston, who had been photographed and feted on the 1st tee of the final round, had never recovered from his missed 30-inch putt on the very first green and, knowing of the Champion's miraculous birdie three at the 2nd, was gone in a welter of strokes. Diegel, however, was tied with the Champion at the 70th hole but while the Champion obtained a birdie four from a bunker, Diegel, from the same bunker, could only escape with a six.

Mac Smith came in through the gathering gloom with a wonderful round of 71, the lowest of that dark and dismal day, but he had started the round six strokes in arrears and that was just too much to spot the Champion and he could not close the gap.

The Champion has now won 11 major championships in the space of seven years. He has passed the record of Mr John Ball, who had won as many in nine, and he has equalled Mr Ball's feat of winning both the Open Championship and Amateur Championship in the same year. Without detracting in any way from the great field assembled at Hoylake, the Champion won with his game far from its peak.

I began this piece by stating that I felt a sense of wonderment and awe at the Champion's success. The wonderment stems from a victory obtained in spite of playing under a tight rein. The awe stems from what may happen now that the Champion stands with his flag firmly planted on two sides of the Impregnable Quadrilateral. Two more sides remain at Interlachen and then

Merion. Can he do it? If destiny has its way, then I believe he can.

Footnote: The 1980 Open Championship marks the 50th anniversary of the second leg of Bobby Jones' incomparable feat of winning the Open Championships and the Amateur Championships of Britain and America. Throughout his career, Jones' feats on the golf course were gracefully reported for the *Atlanta Journal* and the *American Golfer* magazine by Oscar Bane Keeler, known to all as O.B. Keeler died in 1950 and Jones died in 1971. This article is a tribute to both.
(1980)

THE PUTT THAT CHEERED

It was only a little putt; I mean it was a putt that you or I, on most occasions, would have knocked away, picked up or kicked grudgingly towards the opposition. Admittedly, it was for the match and if it had been one of my twitch-ridden opponents I most certainly would have wanted to see it disappear, but at the standard I'm talking about, it appeared to be a foregone conclusion.

When professional golfers of the standing of Craig Stadler have a short putt to win a Ryder Cup four-ball match, then foregone conclusions are usually the order of the day. When professional golfers of Craig Stadler's standing actually miss such a short putt then the repercussions can be catatonic. Apart from feeling a twinge of sympathy for any locker-room door which happened to come within range of Mr Stadler's boot, I admit I had to stifle a most unsportsmanlike shout of delight when Mr Stadler's ball stayed out.

All right, I can hear you saying, so Stadler missed the putt to give us a fortunate half instead of a loss but there was still a day and a half to go, the scores were still tied and the Americans were right in it. All of which is true but does not take into account the devastating blow to American morale which that putt engendered. From being two points ahead after the first day foursomes, one point ahead at the end of the first day, the Americans had struggled in the second day morning four-balls to lose two and win one with one match still out on the course. When Curtis Strange laid his second shot to the 16th stone dead for a two up lead, it looked odds on the Americans retaining their one point lead at lunch. Sandy Lyle provided the first jolt to their complacency when he holed a monster eagle putt across the 17th green to claw one back but even though both Lyle and Bernhard Langer hit the 18th green in two, they were joined by Stadler. Then came that putt and the Americans were in disarray.

Conversely, the Europeans were in a state of euphoria for not only did they find themselves on terms, they had also been provided with a conclusive demonstration of American fallibility. When they emerged for the second day foursomes they set about the opposition in a manner which brooked no argument and stamped their authority on the destiny of that elegant gold trophy.

The mood was still upon the Europeans for the final day singles, not least because Tony Jacklin had proved himself a far superior tactician in his line-up than Lee Trevino. Admittedly, Jacklin was dealing from a position of strength while Trevino had no choice but to lead off with his big guns, but Jacklin foresaw this probability and placed his strong men in the upper middle of the order, reckoning perhaps that even if Europe did lose two of the first three matches, the teams would still only be tied and Messrs Ballesteros, Lyle and Langer would do the business. As it turned out, it all went horribly wrong for Trevino when first Manuel Pinero dealt with Lanny Wadkins and then Paul Way saw off Ray Floyd. Even though Ian Woosnam had lost to Stadler, this meant that the Americans had to win seven of the remaining nine singles to win the Cup and there was little possibility of that.

So a great and glorious day passed with patriotic cheers ringing round the course as the Europeans rose to the occasion. Ballesteros, who has yet to win a Ryder Cup single in three attempts, salvaged his pride with three birdies in the last five holes to gain a half with Tom Kite, Sandy Lyle produced some of the best golf of the day to beat Peter Jacobsen in a thoroughly sporting encounter, Bernhard Langer was merciless in his destruction of hapless Hal Sutton, Howard Clark was all Yorkshire grit in his defeat of Mark O'Meara and and it was left to tearful Sam Torrance to administer the *coup de grâce* on luckless Andy North. But on that final afternoon they were all heroes, for even those players who eventually lost were hounding their opponents to a degree that must have provided inspiration to their fellows.

It was an uncharacteristically subdued Lee Trevino who provided his last press conference and even he could only fall back on the lame excuse that the Europeans holed more long putts than his men, and that the greens were too slow. Maybe he had forgotten that putting is part of the game just like driving and iron-play, and we outplayed the Americans in those departments as well. As for the much-vaunted unsportsmanlike behaviour by the crowd and the references to hissing at American wives, that is all so much baloney. British sports crowds do not hiss, it's not in our national makeup. The plain facts are that the Americans could not stomach the notion of defeat and the whingeing from such players as Floyd and Sutton does them no good at all. Having stood on various vantage points on various courses and watched the Americans win the Ryder Cup, the Walker Cup, the Curtis Cup and any other Cup on offer, I have absolutely no sympathy for them. They were beaten and beaten comprehensively and who can blame the European golf supporter for enjoying such rarely tasted fruits of victory? For Tony Jacklin it was a triumph and perhaps a small measure of revenge for the unspeakable things Trevino did to him in 1972. For the European players it was the final proof that they are a force to be reckoned with anywhere in the world. For the Americans it was a chastening reminder that the rest of the world has caught up with them.

There is no doubt in my mind that the Ryder Cup will, in the future, serve plenty of time on this side of the Atlantic. The next step is to go over there and win it. For the time being, however, let us content ourselves with the memories of The Belfry with perhaps a small suggestion for a commemorative plaque by the side of the 18th green, roughly in line with Stadler's putt. On it should read the inscription: "Here lies the myth of American invincibility. Buried 15th September, 1985."
(1985)

AN OPEN REMEMBERED

The captains and the kings have long since departed Muirfield, where Tom Watson wooed his lady love of Lothian in a manner which left all the other suitors still standing in the parlour, hoping that the fickle mistress of Kent will bestow her favours upon them next year.

It was a good Championship but certainly not a great one for it lacked the drama and passion with which the event has been associated in past years.

This was due to a final round in which Watson clinically dissected the course with a display of remorseless, almost mechanical golf, the efficiency of which put him beyond the grasp of his nearest challengers. But like all Championships, this one had its moments and the first of these occurred on the second day when one man made light of the conditions and caused a few splutters among the Honourable Company of Edinburgh Golfers.

The name of Horacio Carbonetti is hardly household but this 32-year-old Argentinian had an enchanted morning with his putter and after using it only

28 times posted a 64. Carbonetti, who was nicknamed "Carburettor" by some wag because he played that round at full throttle, needed such a score, for after an opening 78 he was in danger of missing the halfway cut. Alas for him, his mixture was too rich on the third day, and with a flood of strokes he went back to another 78 and was on the road home.

The second round was also the day that Jack Nicklaus thrust himself into the reckoning with a 67 and, on hearing that the great man had reached the turn in 32 and could conceivably tie or beat the new record, Herbert Warren Wind, the eloquent New Yorker writer, wryly remarked: "Nicklaus is good, but he is no Carbonetti."

Lee Trevino also produced a second round 67 to take the lead and then revealed some dietary secrets. That morning Trevino had gone against his normal practice and eaten a full breakfast of eggs, sausages and toast and tea. He usually didn't eat anything before playing as he had an old saying: "A hungry dog hunts best." But following that 67, he found he had another saying: "If you have a full stomach, butterflies have no room there." All of which was rather alimentary, my dear Trevino.

Back to the Carbonetti 64, in which this former lawyer was asked by the world's press to go through his round stroke by stroke. On describing the 13th, a puzzled look crossed his face, at which point John Redmond of the Irish Press, chairman of the Irish Golf Writers and noted wit, remarked: "That was the hole you obviously didn't play."

If the Honourable Company spluttered over that course record, they positively choked on the third day, for not only was that record beaten, it was beaten by a Japanese. During the Second World War, James Logan, the head greenkeeper at Muirfield, had fallen into Japanese hands but it is doubtful if he ever imagined the record of his cherished course following suit.

Fall it did to Isao Aoki, he of the alarming swing and toe in the air putting stroke. Aoki weaved his own spell of Oriental magic on the greens, rationing himself to 24 putts and 39 other strokes to tie Mark Hayes' Championship record of 1977. Aoki's round was perfect in its symmetry, containing nine threes and nine fours and his only disappointment came when he was told afterwards that if he had scored one stroke less he would have won £50,000 for a new record, offered by the American magazine Golf. Mark you, that same magazine had already been hit by both Aoki and Nicklaus, for they offered a similar sum to anyone who broke the US Open aggregate record.

The evolvement of Aoki's putting style came about some 10 years ago when he borrowed a putter which happened to be much longer than his normal blade. As he naturally carried his hands low on all his shots, Aoki decided to do the same with the putter and so the legend began. Although his English is still rather limited, he surprised everyone when he suddenly remarked: "It's my trademark!"

Further questioning through an interpreter revealed that Aoki is still undecided what to do about the house he won last year for his hole-in-one at the Suntory World Match-Play Championship. The absentee landlord of Gleneagles has never even bothered to collect the keys and commented sadly, again in perfect English: "It's the tax."

There was a moment of sadness too as Arnold Palmer departed the Championship at the halfway stage. It is 20 years since he made his first appearance at St Andrews and he seemed doubtful if he would ever play in it again. If any man made the Championship what it is today it is Palmer, for he was the first of the Americans to preach the gospel that no man could consider his career complete without an Open Championship to his name. In Palmer's wake, others followed, and when he won in 1961 and 1962, the trickle of American entrants became a torrent.

His chief regret was that he hadn't won in 1960 when he was already the winner of the US Masters and US Open. That year, the final round on the last day was rained out.

"I did not believe there was any way I could lose if we had gone on that afternoon," said Palmer in a departing interview. "When I first came over I found everything as I expected it to be – the atmosphere and the tradition were there. Over the years there have been many changes but I hope that however successful the Championship gets in the years ahead it doesn't lose some of the things I thought were really great. In other words, let's not make it a sideshow and forget what's happening in the centre of the ring. That would be very bad and would spoil what is a great Championship and it will get greater still as long as golf is not left on the sidelines."

It is unlikely that will ever happen but the Royal and Ancient, who now run what is ostensibly the biggest multi-sponsored event in the world, would do well to heed Palmer's warning if we are to continue to cherish the moments this great Championship provides.

(1980)

Ryderwatch

A strange phenomenon will descend on the country today. Instead of the usual Sunday afternoon activities, the nation will be gripped in a kind of paralysis.

Lawns will go unmown, cars unwashed and the dogs unwalked. Pubs will resemble the Marie Celeste, golf courses will be equally deserted, sermons will be delivered to empty pews and anyone travelling on a motorway will find it devoid of traffic.

Yes, at approximately 1.30 pm Hurricane Ryder will sweep across the land leaving a trail of domestic devastation as every golfer will be rooted in front of the television to watch the finale from Kiawah Island. In order to enjoy the virtually continuous seven-hour coverage promised, certain preparations have to be made.

First it must be made clear to any visiting relatives that unless they are golfers, they should not expect any contributions from you on any subject unless it concerns the Ryder Cup.

Equally, children and pets should be banished from the room. This has been a house rule since the dog was ill at the climax of the semi-final between England and West Germany in last year's World Cup and neither of my children made a move to help.

Prior agreement should be made with the management for a plentiful supply of food and beverages and a shift system should be initiated so that these are delivered at the appropriate times.

Now that you are ensconced in your favourite armchair in the privacy of your own home, you can exhibit varying degrees of appalling patriotism in a manner you would't dream of at any other time.

This is your opportunity to cheer unreservedly when one of our brave lads wins a hole and applaud with equal vigour when one of theirs misses a putt. You can leap to your feet and cry "you're the man" as Ballesteros rips into another drive and "get in the hole" as Woosnam blasts an iron shot to a short hole. This is no time to subdue national fervour, we want our chaps to win, hopefully by as large a margin as possible.

Of course, during such a protracted broadcast there will be moments of relative inaction when nothing much seems to be happening. These can be filled by playing a new indoor game which I have just patented, called "Cliché Golf". It works like this: every time you hear a well-worn phrase or saying from one of the commentators on the play of a particular hole, you can award yourself a birdie. Two clichés and it's an eagle.

Expressions to listen out for are "he'll he disappointed with that", "he'll be hoping to hole this", and "he has this for a birdie" when the putt in question is more than 40 feet long, downhill on a lightning-fast green with three breaks.

On this basis I have to report that if I hadn't fallen asleep for the final two holes, I would have comfortably broken 60 at St Pierre in the last round of the Epson Grand Prix a week ago.

One must consider the remote possibility that Europe may lose. To avoid any wanton destruction in this event, all small breakable items in the room should be removed beforehand and the cat should make itself scarce. It might also be advisable to lay on a couple of chaps in white coats armed with suitable restraining gear.

Whatever happens, it will be a draining experience which is likely to leave you tired and emotional for some time afterwards. So whether it's celebration or commiseration, just be grateful it happens only every two years. (1991)

PASS THE SPONGE

A golfing friend of mine has a novel and refreshing way of venting his feelings on that inanimate object which occupies the corner of his living-room, the television set.

Since most of us have at one time or another experienced an almost irresistible urge to heave a brick through the offending screen, my friend's solution has universal appeal. Being in the plastic foam business, he has provided himself with a supply of sponge bricks in a variety of colours.

Prior to the recent General Election he had armed himself with a number of these bricks in blue, red and yellow and whenever something or someone particularly irritating appeared he selected the appropriate colour and hurled it forcefully at the picture. This, he informed me, afforded him immense satisfaction as well as saving on the repair costs he would have incurred had he used the real thing.

Following the truncated broadcast of the final round of the British Masters tournament, my friend told me that he had rarely experienced greater frustration and that his floor looked like the bath-house at Pompeii might have looked just before Vesuvius became unplayable.

No doubt the BBC will provide a reason for leaving the viewers stranded with the tournament incomplete, but whatever the excuse, there is no doubt that the corporation alienated several million people. It was not as though the next programme was of great urgency since it concerned an alternative comedian warning us of the Earth's environmental problems as part of Earth Summit week.

I appreciate that such problems should be given a full airing, but to continue the golf broadcast for another 20 minutes was not going to have much bearing on the destruction of the rain forests or the perils of global warming. Indeed, the Woburn course looked in such splendid condition, with the trees and rhododendrons in full bloom, that it was a first-rate advertisement for man and nature working in harmony.

In the history of televised golf there have been a number of occasions when the broadcast has finished due either to loss of transmission or rigid adherence to schedules. In 1955, when TV golf was in its infancy, coverage of the United States Open was cut just as Jack Fleck lined up his putt to tie Ben Hogan. This so enraged one viewer, a former Walker Cup player, that he hurled an ashtray through the screen.

There was a similar lack of consideration in 1978 when ITV was covering the first European Open at Walton Heath. As Bernard Gallacher walked up to the final hole, needing a four to tie, the transmission was switched to a scheduled children's programme. Gallacher got his untransmitted four but lost the play-off, while ITV lost the allegiance of millions of viewers.

It was in this same tournament that ITV instituted on-course interviews during play. It was not a success, and the failings of this approach were exemplified by this brief conversation between an interviewer and Carl Mason. "What's the toughest shot you have to play over these last four holes?" came the question. Mason looked at the interviewer rather bleakly. "The next one," he replied, "my ball is lying under that bush."

Most viewers believe that on occasions they could do a better job than the commentators. Steve Melnyk, a professional golfer employed by CBS in America, provided ample proof that professionals should stick to playing golf rather than talking about it.

"Peter Jacobsen," said Melnyk, "is in a position where a birdie will help him more than a bogey." Pass the sponge, please.

(1992)

A FEAST TO CAP ANY PREDICTION

Of all the great culinary experiences available *Le filet de chapeau du golf aux pruneaux* is not one which rates a great deal of space in the world's leading cookery books. Having gone into print stating that if Europe didn't win the Ryder Cup I would eat my golf cap there were times, I must confess, when I considered just how I was going to consume this particular accessory. The above recipe was, I felt, somewhat of a master-stroke as the possible indigestibility of the felt and cotton would be eased by the addition of the prunes.

As it turned out, this gastronomic delight was denied me by perhaps the most exciting three days of golf in the history of the game. It is also possible that the game has never been played to such a standard of excellence since the Nicklaus and Watson duel of the 1977 Open Championship but whereas on that occasion there were just two players providing the inspiration, this time there were 24. I cannot remember seeing so many iron shots finishing close to the pin nor so many putts being holed and while in previous Ryder Cups it has been the Americans performing these feats, this time it was us.

In analysing the outcome of any team encounter it is usual to examine the deficiencies in the losing side and no doubt the Americans will be doing just that. It is certain that they will change their method of selection and choose their team on current form during the year of the match rather than including the year before. This may help but it will not cure the root cause of their demise which basically lies in the structure of their Tour. Since the introduction of the all-exempt rule in America, the age of the superstar has passed. No more do the likes of Palmer, Nicklaus, Trevino and Watson bestride the game and the present crop of American players do not have any reputations preceding them. Another major factor is the sheer volume of money available, not all of it for winning tournaments. Such is the excess of sideshow events connected to the Tour that it is quite possible to make a handsome living without actually winning a tournament. Nothing breeds confidence like a victory and the more victories, the greater the aura of invincibility.

Stripped of this aura, the Americans were struggling against a team which had been bred on consistent success throughout the season. What confidence the Americans may have had was severely dented during the first series of foursomes when they were up in all four games and only won two with the heaviest psychological blow being struck by Woosnam and Faldo's recovery from four down.

This undermining of American confidence produced a complete subsidence in the four-balls when the Europeans produced a brand of golf which was not really of this world, and when we continued in the same vein on the second day, the unimaginable looked a distinct possibility.

In spite of Europe's five point lead at this stage, I still had the golf cap marinating quietly in the pantry for I had witnessed too many American recoveries in the past. Their counter-attack produced the most nerve-racking two hours I have ever experienced but in the end European resilience prevailed. All our players were heroes but special mention should go to Eamonn Darcy, whose vital win against Crenshaw turned the match in our favour. To go into the history books as the man who lost the Ryder Cup playing against an opponent who had broken his putter would have destroyed anyone. Not that Crenshaw putted badly but no putt was ever more important or difficult than the one Darcy holed on the final green to win. I would think that he still wakes up in the middle of the night in a cold sweat at the thought of it.

Severiano Ballesteros looked a different man – ebullient and inspirational, he was doing what he enjoys most, that is knocking the stuffing out of Americans. Whether he heard Lanny Wadkins sounding off about Curtis Strange being the best golfer in the world because Strange has won $700,000 this year I do not know, but Ballesteros certainly played like a man who was going to ram that statement down everybody's throat. In the end it was European resolve on the final hole which won the day and American inexperience which lost it with Dan Pohl and Larry Mize both collapsing at the vital moment and Larry Nelson being totally conned into a half by Bernhard Langer on the last green. No praise can be too high for the captaincy of Tony Jacklin, who appeared to be in several places at the same time and whose passion for victory far outweighed the responses of his counterpart. The Europeans were magnificent in giving all of us a sense of pride and all I can add is that in such an emotional and tense finish, should I have had to eat the golf cap, the prunes would have been entirely unnecessary.
(1987)

PLAYER: THE MASTER WHO IS STILL LEARNING

The ability to learn from one's mistakes on the golf course is considered of prime importance in the making of a golfer. The ability to remember those mistakes and not make them again was the key to Gary Player's stunning victory in the 42nd United States Masters.

Player first played at Augusta in 1957 and missed the cut. In the ensuing years he won the title in 1961 and 1974, but in 1978 he attributed his win not to what he had learnt from victory but to what he had remembered from defeat. In 1962, the year he lost the play-off to Arnold Palmer, he had a putt from behind the hole on the 16th and, hitting it on the right-hand edge of the hole, saw the ball stay out. Again in 1970 he came to the last hole needing a par to tie Gene Littler and Billie Casper and in going for the pin saw his ball catch the lip of the bunker from where he failed to get down in two more.

In the closing stages of Sunday's last round Player once more found himself directly behind the hole on the 16th and this time told himself to hit the ball straight at the back of the hole. Similarly on the 18th he faced a downhill putt on exactly the same line as he had in 1970. On both previous occasions he missed but this time he did not. The fact that Player holed those two vital putts as well as several others was the result of a definite change in his putting stroke.

"Last week," Player said, "I decided to change my putting method. For years I have jabbed at the ball and although I have been playing well I haven't been holing the putts. My caddie asked me to try and hit the ball with more of a stroking action. Although I hit the ball really well during the first three rounds the putts still didn't fall, but on the last day it all paid off."

But any man who wins over 100 tournaments around the world must be a good putter and Player freely acknowledged that he has had his share of fortune on the greens. At 42 he is the oldest winner of the Masters and it is his capacity to adapt and adjust that has kept him at the top for 20 years. He may seem slightly fanatical, even eccentric, but one cannot take away the fact that his exercising, his rigid training schedule and his balanced diet are all important cornerstones in the structuring of his career.

Although Hubert Green's missed putt on the final green will be the lasting memory of his run at the title it should be remembered that on such a day a score of 72 was really about two over par and he was the first to admit it. There were echoes of Doug Sanders at St Andrews in 1970 when Green stood over his 3ft putt and then stepped away. Apparently he heard a radio announcer relaying the situation back to base, but as soon as he did step back one could almost sense he would not hole that putt.

Of course in the tumult of such a finish a great many other things tend to pass unnoticed. There was Severiano Ballesteros, who on his 21st birthday had a sad round but was still full of attacking strokes. His impetuosity cost him dear throughout the week but he is not going to change immediately, and indeed why should he? There was a gratifying performance from Peter Oosterhuis, who at one stage on the last day was in fact ahead of Player, and Peter McEvoy, although propping up the field at the end, could take comfort in the fact that he completed the full four rounds, something no other English amateur had done previously.

The lasting memory, however, should rightly belong to the winner. For me it was the sight of Player hitting his second shot to the 13th in the final round. After the ball was struck Player's right shoulder came swinging round and he nearly fell over such was the effort he put into the stroke.

It is a sight that we have become familiar with over the past 20 years whenever Player has been in the thick of the battle. It signifies the intensity of his desire to win, a desire that enabled him to pass no fewer than 16 men in the course of the final round. The following morning he was back on the course playing with his son, Wayne, and teaching him the intricacies of Augusta National, most of it no doubt from memory.
(1978)

THROUGH THE WRINGER AGAIN

The thousands of bleary-eyed golfers who shuffled into work on the Monday morning following the Masters acted as eloquent testimony to how the nation was gripped by the remarkable victory of Sandy Lyle.

No matter that Lyle himself is more than a millionaire and his individual security is assured, his triumph was for Britain and proof that British players can produce the goods. Not that Lyle allowed us any moments of quiet contemplation of an anticipated victory.

Three of his previous four wins in America were achieved after sudden-death play-offs, his 1985 Open title was completed with an agonising effort on the final hole and now he has put us all through the wringer once more.

But it was worth it. His play over the last three holes when he was really under the cosh was just about the bravest finish I've ever witnessed.

It is impossible to convey to anyone who has not played Augusta just how fast the putt from behind the hole at the 16th is, nor is it made any easier by a savage left to right slope.

Once the ball is set in motion, the only way it can be stopped from rolling off the green is for it to hit the back of the hole and disappear. To actually pull off this impossible trick to tie the lead on the 70th hole of the Masters is a feat almost beyond comprehension. Then, having buoyed our spirits up, he sent them plunging down again when he drove into a bunker at the last.

Fortunately, bunkers at Augusta are not the lotteries that one tends to find in this country and, unless a ball plugs, a good lie is invariably assured. In Lyle's case it was a question of how near to the lip the ball lay.

As it had come to rest slightly on the upslope he knew he could get the height required to carry the ball over the bunker in front of the green. Also, if he made clean contact, he would impart just that little more backspin and maybe bring the ball back down the slope to the pin. For a player of his calibre, the shot itself was not too difficult; it was the situation that was fraught with peril, but he rose to the occasion splendidly and executed the stroke to perfection. The putt he had left is extremely deceptive because it looks like a right lip putt but it is in fact straight.

I remember Gary Player saying in 1978, when he faced a longer putt on the same line for his ultimately winning round of 64, that he had missed that putt before by thinking it was on the right edge. Would Lyle read it correctly? He most certainly did and I'm sure I heard the collective sigh of relief from those who were foregoing their sleep.

Not only was it a magnificent victory, it was a case of justice being seen to be done. It would have been a travesty if Lyle had lost his Masters and it would have been an extreme embarrassment to American golf if Mark Calcavecchia had won.

Mr Calcavecchia is probably a very pleasant person and it is not his fault that he has a swing like a hod-carrier. That he has courage there is no doubt, for his holing out over the final nine holes was resolute and flawless.

No, the embarrassment would have lain in the method by which he got his ball to arrive on the green, for Calcavecchia plays a make of golf club that has been designated non-conforming by the USGA because the width of the grooves exceeds the measurements laid down.

Because of the large number of these clubs currently in circulation, any amateur golfer has until 1996 to rid him or herself of these implements. At the start of the 1990 season, no professional golfer can play in a tournament using this particular type of club but, and this is a big but, any professional tournament committee currently has the right to ban these clubs from its tournament right now.

Since the Masters tournament committee is not answerable to any governing body in terms of how it runs its tournament, it could have, and should have, banned these clubs from the Masters. If Calcavecchia had won it would have left a very sour taste indeed.

Finally, no Masters would be complete without the Hord Hardin show. A graduate of the Ronald Reagan School of Lucid Response, old Hard of Hearin' wound up the proceedings with a memorable display of ineptitude.

First, he congratulated Jay Sigel for finishing as leading amateur while the new champion, who finished 19 strokes ahead of Sigel, was left to stew. Then Hardin couldn't remember the name of the new Masters champion and then he began wittering on about Sandy having 15 clubs in his bag.

For a moment Lyle looked stunned, as well he might as the prospect of disqualification for having too many clubs loomed. However, it transpired that Hardin was referring to 'patience' being Sandy's 15th club. While all this was going on a technician could clearly be seen scrambling around on the floor – maybe he was looking for Hardin's missing brain.

In the meantime we can all bask in the reflected glory of Sandy Lyle's marvellous achievement and yet another chapter in golf's latest best-seller "The Rise and Rise of British and European Golf."
(1988)

WHY SQUABBLERS ROOST WANTED THE RYDER CUP

To: Lord Derby, Chairman, Ryder Cup Committee
From: The Captain, Squabblers Roost Golf Club

My Lord,

At the last Club Committee Meeting it was decided that, even at this late stage, it was worth writing to you to submit the name of Squabblers Roost Golf Club to the list of potential venues for the 1993 Ryder Cup.

It may well be that you have never heard of Squabblers Roost, or to give it its full name, Squabblers Roost New Town Old Links. But it has an impressive history, dating as far back as 1961, and has staged many international encounters.

The last one, the annual clash between the English and Scottish members of the club, again found the English members totally out-numbered, and it was only by enlisting sundry Welsh and Irish, plus the token Jewish member, that a match of equal numbers could be arranged. Needless to say, the Scots lost again.

Let's be frank, Your Lordship, we intend to put Squabblers Roost on the map. After all, no one would have heard of The Belfry if it hadn't been for the Ryder Cup and, since every course in the country seems to have applied to stage it, in many cases to earn some cheap publicity, then we don't see why we shouldn't do the same. (What's more, we can't have these foreigners taking the match over, can we?)

Not that we aren't a worthy venue. Like all clubs, we acknowledge that our biggest asset is the course itself, and we are prepared to spare no expense to bring it up to the right conditions. You may feel that at 5,900 yards it is a little short by today's standards, but the course record is only 59 against a par of 66, and the fans like to see low scores nowadays.

Some of the holes are really tricky, particularly those round the turn near the motorway intersection – the sight of a multiple pile-up has spoilt many a good card, I can tell you.

It's difficult to say which school of course architecture was responsible for the design of Squabblers Roost. Some of the members say "Early Municipal", but I feel there is a hint of Trent Jones in the use of the open-cast mine which forms the main feature of the 1st hole, while the disused railway line, which has to be crossed six times in play, shows the influence of Pete Dye – all the sleepers are missing.

The 18th is a really good finishing hole: the motorway is out of bounds on the right and, although you can hook the tee shot on to the adjoining 17th fairway, it makes the second shot, which is blind anyway, that much more difficult. The green is set on a mound, and slopes from front to back, and at 345 yards, usually downwind, it's been the scene of much drama in the past.

Accommodation should be no problem, as all of us at the club will be only too pleased to put up a team member each. In fact, our lady captain would be happy to take two, but if I were you I'd make sure they were Americans – we want our lads fresh on the 1st tee, if you get my drift.

On the catering side, our steward and stewardess have plenty of experience with the many societies that visit the club and you will find them most co-operative.

One small point: the President, the Secretary, the Professional and myself are all prepared to give up our car-parking spots in the club car park, so that you and the other dignitaries have free access.

I think that covers most of the main items, although I realise that there are several other details, such as car-parking for 20,000 vehicles, tented village, victory banquet, etc., which I have not covered.

Once we get the contract, however, these can be ironed out. All in all, and considering the infighting over the venue, we believe that Squabblers Roost would be a most appropriate choice.

Yours sincerely,
Arthur Plunge, Captain,
Squabblers Roost Golf Club
(1990)

DREAMING ALONG THE PRO–AM TRAIL

Of all the games men and women play, and leaving aside the most obvious, only golf provides the opportunity for the ordinary player to play alongside the game's finest and, on occasions, improve on their score.

As golf has attracted greater interest, so the pro-am has become an integral part of the professional game, providing amateurs with that superior feeling of role-playing other amateur sports men and women can never attain.

So what is it really like playing in a pro-am? Is it fun or is it a nightmare? To a large extent it depends on how well you play, but however good you are you will quickly discover that your professional plays an entirely different game to the one you and I attempt to play.

The vast distances he hits the ball means that he can become a very remote figure, striding out ahead of you, oblivious to the ineffectual hacks you are perpetrating behind him. You will meet him on each tee and each green, but otherwise contact is minimal.

It will probably come as no surprise to you to learn that we who earn what is laughably called a living writing about the game receive our fair share of invitations to play in pro-ams. Such invitations have dubious benefits. While we enjoy playing with the professionals, we are acutely aware of the damage that can occur to our reputations for being knowledgeable and erudite about the game.

The facts are that just because we write about golf doesn't necessarily mean we are any good at it. Quite the contrary. We spend our days watching the professionals playing considerably better than we ever shall and, since the tournament scene takes in most of the summer months, our forays on to the course are limited to days when the wind is coming in direct from the Urals and our fingers are liable to severe attacks of frostbite.

Playing in pro-ams is not for the faint-hearted and waiting to drive off the 1st tee is considered, by some amateurs, as the finest laxative in the world. This strain can be avoided if you adopt my personal high-tension preparations.

First, leave your house at the height of the rush hour. This will ensure that you are trapped in a colossal traffic jam and will probably arrive at the course five minutes before you are due to tee off.

On arrival, grab all your gear from the car and rush to the changing room. While changing, tug especially hard on your shoe laces as snapping one at this juncture will keep your mind off the ordeal ahead of you. Next, rush out to the tee but try to tip all your clubs and a few balls in the car park. When you get to the tee, smile briefly at your partners and then attempt to repair the shoe lace.

Whatever you do, don't take any practice swings. Fate always decrees that your name is called on last in the order of striking. So after your professional has boomed his drive 250 yards down the fairway, and the other amateurs have also driven, you should by now be in a state of total anguish, which will be reflected in the speed of your swing. You will either miss the ball altogether or hit a screamer down the middle.

If there's one golden rule to remember about pro-am golf it is always to retain your sense of humour and don't let anything upset you. Accidents can happen even before you've struck a shot in anger, particularly when your name comes to be announced by the starter.

The Americans love this announcement angle. At one pro-am in Florida, Clive Clark was due to tee off. Unfortunately, whoever had written Clive's name on the starting sheet had been a little over-zealous with the C of his first name. The starter took the microphone: "And now from London, England, that well-known professional Olive Clark." No prizes for guessing what Clive's nickname is now.

With a name like mine the mis-spellings are legion. The prize, however, goes to another American announcer who, on seeing my name on the list, spoke out thus: "And now, folks, a very special treat for all you movie fans, the very talented and personable star of the *Sound of Music*... Christopher Plummer!"

On reflection, one of the songs from that film could serve as the amateur golfer's hymn. I'm sure you know the one I mean – it goes something like this: "Climb every mountain, ford every stream, follow every fairway till you find your dream."

And dreams are what pro-am golf is all about.

(1978)

Non-Battle for the Top

There has been a dramatic new development in the battle for world supremacy between Nick Faldo and Greg Norman. After a great deal of jostling for position, both players have hit upon the same scheme for staying on top of the Sony Rankings.

Having slaved through the season, winning two major championships en route, Faldo has found he was still lying second to the man he had totally outplayed at St Andrews. Shortly after the Open, however, Faldo leapt from his bath and with a cry of "Mark McCormack" found he had the answer.

"Obviously," he reasoned, "I cannot be number one through the accuracy of my tee shots, the incisiveness of my irons, or the quality of my short game, but there is more than one way to skin a wombat."

Carefully calculating the complicated averaging system of the Rankings, Faldo reached the conclusion that the less he played the more likely his position would improve. It was a master stroke. In a few weeks of relative inactivity he had overtaken Norman at the top and seemed destined to stay there.

However, the country which spawned Kylie Minogue is not without its intellectual giants. Within a matter of days Norman had also adopted a policy of not playing and with a superb display of non-shot-making clawed his way back to the top.

There could be a message for all of us in this. If we apply ourselves as diligently to not playing, then surely we, too, could achieve similar status. Of course to become a truly great non-player you would need to dedicate yourself to the task.

It would be no good not playing for a couple of weeks and then succumbing to the urge to take your clubs on to the course. Instead you must plan your non-playing schedule carefully and measure your success gradually.

There will be many distractions. Your family, on seeing you at home at the weekend, may think you are free for domestic chores, but if you maintain your non-playing cocoon of concentration then the sky's the limit. The club championship will be a formality, followed by county honours, an international appearance and then the Walker Cup in which every other year, Great Britain will not play the Americans over here and the Americans will not play us over there.

After the Walker Cup you will face the biggest decision of your non-playing life – do you become a non-playing professional? The transition will not be easy. First you will have to get through the non-playing qualifying school and if successful, make the cut in the big non-playing tournaments. Competition will be fierce and standards much higher.

It will be no good just sitting around and not playing only at weekends – non-playing professional golf requires the daily regime of not hitting thousands of practice balls, of endless hours of not working on your short game.

The rewards are there for the taking and you could become the first man to win the four major championships in a single year – known collectively as the non-Slam.

Yes, non-playing golf could be the answer for all of us who have ever tried to play the game. It would remove the frustration and bad temper which follows a foozled stroke, it would eliminate slow play, leave courses uncrowded and save on expensive maintenance.

The role of the club professional would remain unaffected as he would still give a non-playing lesson and books and magazines would flourish with advice on how famous players tackled difficult non-playing situations.

This Utopian state of affairs would mean that more and more people would want to join clubs as non-playing members and consequently bar and catering profits would soar. Then the Rules of Golf would be reduced to one simple statement: "The ball must not be played as it lies."

One thing we would not need in our non-playing environment would be a points system defining the best non-player at any given time. We've already got that in the Sony Rankings.
(1990)

THE AGE OF AQUA GOLF

"Water," as W C Fields is reputed to have said, "is dangerous stuff – fish make love in it." Whatever fish do get up to beneath the surface, if they are located anywhere near a recently constructed golf course they will be doing it to a constant bombardment of golf balls.

This is the era of aqua golf. The age when a golfer is judged not by the number of strokes taken but by the number of balls left in the bag at the end of the round. Influenced by the scenic qualities of Augusta, whose second nine holes could be regarded as the Venice of championship golf, architects are literally flooding the game with artificial lakes, streams, ponds and in some cases waterfalls. In the last two US PGA championships, played respectively at Oak Tree and Kemper Lakes, it was a case of "spot the fairway" as golf balls were launched over vast stretches of water towards some distant island green, while in the background jets of spray spouted forth from fountains set in the middle of a lake. One almost expected a school of trained dolphins to leap from the water in response to each ball that passed overhead.

Clearly this is a case of overkill, or overspill, if you like. Architects have gone overboard in their attempts to build so-called championship courses which may play host to the professionals for one week in the year. For the other 51 weeks the ordinary player is left to reflect miserably on the disappearance of yet another ball into the depths.

Working on the assumption that if it is to do with golf and it comes from America it must be good, it is almost obligatory for any new course in Britain to be strewn with water hazards. Practically every glossy brochure for a new course which finds its way into my wastepaper basket is extolling the virtues of American-type courses in the heart of the British countryside. Even the names of some of them confirm the trans-Atlantic influence. The Quietwaters club in Essex leaves you in no doubt what to expect when you play there, while there is a whiff of unilateralism about the East Sussex National course near Uckfield. If you can let me know when East Sussex seceded from the realm I would be grateful.

Golf is enough of a challenge without the need for additional aquatic sport. The classic links courses which stage the Open Championship have got by for centuries with the minimum of water. Carnoustie's Barry Burn, even though the course is not on the rota at the moment, makes the 17th and 18th pretty terrifying, but still eminently fair. The burn in front of the 16th at Turnberry gathers a number of balls as does the 14th at Royal St George's, but undoubtedly the most pernicious trickle of all is the Swilcan Burn at St Andrews. Scene of numerous tragi-comedies, the Swilcan has lapped up golf balls struck by the highest and the lowest.

It is as the 19th hole in a matchplay event that the Swilcan causes the greatest anguish. In the 1895 Amateur Championship, the unfortunate trio of William Greig, Lawrie Auchterlonie and John Ball all departed from the tournament in extra-time by finding the water. Fate twisted the knife a little further for the sole beneficiary of this catalogue of disaster was Leslie Balfour-Melville, who won his last three matches, including the final, as a result. Perhaps the definitive story regarding the Swilcan concerns the man who, playing the hole as the 19th in a match, fluffed into the water three times. It is said that he first threw his clubs in, then his caddie and finally himself.

One other Scottish water hazard caught the eye of an Ulster professional as he was flying into Edinburgh Airport for the first time. As the aircraft circled the city the professional looked out of the window, turned to his companion and inquired: "What's that stretch of water down there?" "That's the Forth" came the reply. "Jaysus!" said the Irishman, "that's a hell of a carry." (1990)

Never Complain and Never Explain

If you walked into a country club in America and suggested a game of Scotch foursomes, as they call it, they would look at you as though you had just arrived from another planet.

On the other hand, most British club golfers would declare that foursomes are possibly the best form of golf and certainly preferable to the deeply tedious four-ball.

With such a disparity in the popularity of foursomes between the two nations it is hard to come to terms with the first morning debacle in the Walker Cup match at Portmarnock. For the second time in four years the home team was whitewashed in the first set of foursomes, thereby making the final outcome of the contest virtually a foregone conclusion. Why should this be so? Why should a form of golf which is part of the game's heritage in these islands provide such a dismal record?

Peter McEvoy, a veteran of five Walker Cup matches but a significant absentee in 1987 and this time, believes that it is purely a case of nerves. "The Walker Cup *is* amateur golf," says McEvoy. "There is far more pressure than playing in the Open or the Masters because there you can lose yourself in the field.

"In the Walker Cup there are 10,000 people milling around and they are watching just four games – there's nowhere to hide. If you haven't experienced that then your nerves can become ragged. The more times you play in the Walker Cup, the easier it is to cope.

"I don't think it's a case of being bad at foursomes, I think the result would be just as bad if we played the singles first with an inexperienced team."

McEvoy has a point, but it is difficult for a captain to put out experienced players when they simply don't exist.

Only Jim Milligan and Garth McGimpsey had played before and even before a ball was struck there had been an unseemly rush to join the professional ranks by four members of the home side immediately the match was over.

Someone who made a close analysis of foursomes play was Diane Bailey, certainly the most successful Curtis Cup captain in recent times and possibly the most thorough captain of any team to emerge from these shores.

She feels that conferring between players is fatal as it creates doubt. "If a player is good enough to get into the team," says Mrs Bailey, "she's good enough to play her own game without her partner interfering.

"I always told my players to play their own game in foursomes and never apologise for a poor shot."

It should be added that Mrs Bailey also made her team play the first three and last three holes in almost endless succession during practice since she realised the importance of a good start and a good finish.

Having taken my summer break for the past 15 years in what I like to call the foursomes capital of the west, namely Trevose in Cornwall, I have realised that there is a considerable art in foursomes play.

The principal rule to follow is that old political maxim "Never complain and never explain". You must assume that your partner is trying and he must think the same of you.

If your partner has put you in the cabbage, you don't want to hear his apologies or how he was put off by the cry of a cormorant at the top of his swing. Your only concern is to get the ball back into play and do it without wittering about the dreadful lie you've got.

The other great advantages of foursomes are the speed you can get round and the fact you are less taxed physically by having to play only half the shots.

Provided each member of the side is on hand immediately to play the second shot from the partner's drive (another of Diane Bailey's essentials as it prevents conferring), then a reasonably competent foursome should get round in a little over two hours.

Having to play only half the shots can create psychological problems since you can play several holes without having to hole a short putt.

Suddenly you have "one of those" and the temptation to complain and explain is almost unbearable. This must be resisted, for if it is not then it is almost certain you will miss it.

Maybe Walker Cup foursomes are not quite the friendly, social affairs they are at club level, but I still find it amazing that we should lose so consistently to a nation which never plays this form of golf.

There is a story which illustrates this concerning an American playing in the match for the first time who was somewhat confused by the captain's briefing on the alternate shot format for the foursomes. "Does this mean," he asked, "that if my guy holes out last I have to drive off from the next tee?" (1991)

CLOWN PRINTS

I am very worried about my relationship with Payne Stewart. I mean, the man has a swing you would sell your grandmother for, he drives the ball long and reasonably straight, and chips and putts beautifully.

True, there's a slight question mark concerning his resistance to sustained pressure, but overall he is an exceptionally gifted golfer, a multi-millionaire and a pleasant fellow with a nice wife and a couple of kids. Yet every time I see him on the golf course I have this irresistible urge to collapse with laughter.

The trouble is that Stewart dresses like a clown. Whenever he appears on the 1st tee in one of his bizarre outfits I half expect a diminutive stooge to rush out and slap a custard pie in his face or pull out the front of his plus-twos and empty a bucket of water inside them.

The reason why Stewart's sartorial excesses have not been laughed off the course is that we have been led to believe that he brings much needed colour into the game. Well, there's colour and then there's colour. There's colour in terms of charisma and the kind of dash and flair a player brings to golf and then there's colour in terms of the peacock hues that Stewart wears. Unfortunately, particularly among the Americans, there is far too much of the latter and far too little of the former.

Stewart is paid a considerable amount of money to advertise the colours of the teams of the National Football League. But golfers are remembered for the championships they've won, not for promoting the Chicago Bears or the Green Bay Packers.

His outfit on the last day of the Open Championship, when he appeared in a Stars and Stripes shirt, prompted the golf correspondent of the *Glasgow Herald* to remark that Stewart "looked as though he was dressed for burial at sea". When Stewart drove into Coffin Bunker on the 13th to destroy his hopes of catching Nick Faldo, those words took on a prophetic ring.

I have a sneaking suspicion that were Stewart to dress in a more conventional fashion he would disppear among the visored clones who populate the US Tour.

The nearest equivalent to Stewart in Europe is Rodger Davis, as he wears plus-twos and is regarded as a natty dresser. Compared with Stewart, Davis is a model of rectitude whose clothes do very little to offend.

The only items I do find distracting are the socks with his name vertically printed on them. When he first appeared in them about ten years ago I thought his name was Regdor Sivad until I realised I was reading the socks from the feet upwards.

But it has all changed for Davis as he has signed a new clothing contract and will in future be appearing in normal attire. This will not mean that Davis will shrink back into anonymity. Nobody epitomises a nation more than this likeable Australian with a penchant for a few beers and plenty of laughs with his mates plus a few bob on the horses.

The other item of clothing that has been in the news recently is shorts. The question as to whether shorts are suitable attire for golf depends on who's wearing them.

The recent spell of hot weather has contributed to some remarkably revealing garments displayed by several young ladies on various golf courses. Such has been their impact that in some cases the committee has considered invoking a new rule concerning "Movable Distractions".

If, on the other hand, that which is inside the shorts belongs to Brian Barnes then the prospect is less pleasing. Certainly the PGA European Tour think so as they have continued to ban them.

A ban on shorts was brought in three years ago as it was not deemed appropriate wear for professional golfers. When Barnes played in the Open Championship, officialdom raised no objection to him appearing in tailored shorts and long socks.

Clothing for golf has certainly changed in recent years. It is no longer acceptable to turn up at the club on a Sunday morning dressed in the gardener's cast-offs. Nowadays clothing is smart, colourful and a faithful copy of that which is worn by the heroes of the professional game.

This means that spectators at tournaments can dress in the same style as those players they have come to watch. No other sport offers this vicarious form of role-playing. If you want to know which professional a golfer supports just look at the badge on the chest. By their logos, ye shall know them. (1990)

FLIGHTS OF FANTASY

WE'VE NEVER HAD IT SO GOOD

Flinging back the hessian blanket, I leapt from my palliasse at first light, my feet nimbly avoiding the gaps in the floorboards which once had been clad in Axminster.

It was Saturday, which meant it was my turn to crack the ice on the outside water barrel. Although the wind was harsh through what used to be the bedroom window, it troubled me not as I donned my shirt and trousers made from ex-WD blankets. The clothes were a little tight, but after years of being beaten against the rocks in the nearby stream, one expected a little shrinkage and it didn't seem right to grumble when other poor souls were having to scrabble around in the coalsack mountain to find a suitable garment.

My wife was busy in the kitchen standing over the single candle flame preparing breakfast. Like many people, we had taken to hoarding goldfish – the water barrel was full of them – but their mortality rate was high due, in the main, to the next door neighbour's cat.

A few weeks previously we had caught the next door neighbour's cat – and very tasty it was too, if a little stringy – and the fur had made some excellent slippers for the children. Today's breakfast was to be a rare treat – grilled goldfish garnished with bulbs from the garden. The children waited patiently, seated round the tea chest, and their little faces lit up as they tucked in to a tail apiece and squabbled over the last gladioli.

After breakfast we trooped off to the woods to join the other foragers hunting for roots and berries. The woods were crowded and on this particular day there was some unseemly fighting over the carcass of a dead stoat. Frankly, I don't much care for stoat, finding the meat a trifle gamey.

Laden with our pickings from the woods we walked home, pausing briefly at the garage to open the boot of the car, load our roots and berries inside and then open the boot again and take everything out. It's good for the morale to pretend how life used to be and how lucky we are now.

Occasionally, when we are feeling especially low, we get in the car and imagine how it felt to be stuck in a five-mile tailback on the M25, the fumes from the juggernauts filling our lungs.

Being a Saturday, I was going for my usual four-ball at the club and, after a salad of dandelion leaves, I loaded my clubs on to my back, hopped on to my bicycle and clattered off. I say clattered because the tyres from my bike had long since gone – an integral part of a Crisis Casserole my wife discovered in the Government Austerity Cook Book.

The club was two miles away and I arrived half an hour later, rather shaken by the journey but keen to get to grips with the opposition. As I parked the bike, I noticed the richest member of the club had left his Clydesdale horse untethered, so I led him across to the hitching-rail and tied him up next to the captain's donkey.

The course looked in reasonable condition for the time of year, the grass on the fairways was only about knee high and the sheep were managing to keep the grass on the greens at a moderate length. The professional was doing his usual roaring trade in wide-wheeled lawn mowers as every player was obliged to cut a patch in which to place his ball, provided he could find the ball in the first place. I was one of the more fortunate club members, as I possessed a set of steel-shafted clubs and no less than five golf balls. This meant I had no shortage of offers for a game as club and ball sharing had become the rule.

Today, our four-ball would use my Goblin ball which, though well-scuffed, was not actually cut and – since it was my ball – I was allowed to hit it from the 1st tee. We had an enjoyable match, marred only by a brief wrestling match when two of our company both spotted an almost new Spitfire ball at the same time. Afterwards we repaired to the trolley shed where, with the other players, we clustered round the illicit still, cupping our hands to catch the drops of the fiery liquour as they filtered through.

When I arrived home the children were just getting into bed so I was able to read them their favourite story, "Goldilocks and the Squatter Bears". How they laughed when we reached: "Who's been sleeping on my floorboard?" and how they giggled when the father bear said: "Who has been eating my gruel?"

With the children safely tucked up my wife and I sat down to a supper of goldfish kedgeree and then watched the weekly hour of television.

The night's programme featured Match of the Month between Yeovil Town and Northwich Victoria, followed by the Epilogue in which a Trappist monk recounted the parable of the widow's mite using sign language. My wife and I then departed, tired but happy, for bed.

(1992)

A DREAM MATCH-PLAY

Sitting here in my garret, I am faced with the writer's nightmare: the blank sheet of paper that stares mockingly back at me and, rather like a tricky, downhill putt, the longer I look at it the more problems seem to present themselves. Is it possible, I muse, idly raking over some charred rejection slips in the fireplace, to develop a typewriting twitch? Will there come a day when the fingers will remain arched over the keys, unable to move, until by sheer will-power they are plunged down to tap out a demented tattoo that is the writing equivalent of a four-putt green?

It is hot in the garret. The autumn sun streams through the cracked skylight, inducing a feeling of drowsiness. The mind begins to wander and fantasy takes over. Perhaps it is the sight of the leaves turning on the trees or perhaps it is the scent of damp grass but the visions conjured up are those of a russet Wentworth whose fairways run like green ribbons through an October morning mist. It is World Match-Play time and a sense of anticipation is rife among the crowds that move up the hill towards the 1st tee. Eight shiny, black limousines are parked in the forecourt, exclusively available for the players during the week. The flags of the nations represented flutter in the light breeze. On the practice ground, eight figures rifle shots away from the dew-laden grass.

Much controversy arose when the dream World Match-Play field was announced. Writing in *The Times*, Bernard Darwin stated that the event could surely not take place without the presence of Harry Vardon, a man, as that revered scribe once wrote, "whose record is so long it must be severely compressed". But the announcement invoked lively comment in the land and the sponsors sat back, secure in the knowledge that the field they had assembled was unlikely to be beaten by any other eight golfers.

The draw was made and panned out thus: Bobby Jones, three times British Open champion, four times winner of the US Open and perpetrator of the Impregnable Quadrilateral in 1930, was drawn to play Samuel Jackson Snead, three times US Masters winner, three times US PGA winner and 1946 British Open champion. In the second match, Ben Hogan, winner of all golf's major titles and four times US Open champion, is to play Gary Player, five times World Match-Play winner and also winner of all golf's major titles. Match number three brought together Walter Hagen, whose four consecutive US PGA titles between the years 1924-27 marked him as the supreme match player, and Arnold Palmer, twice winner of the World Match-Play, twice winner of the British Open, four times winner of the US Masters and 1960 US Open champion. In the final match, Jack Nicklaus, the man with more major titles to his name than anyone, is due to face Henry Cotton, thrice British Open champion and the man responsible for the elevated status now enjoyed by British professionals.

The starter's voice boomed out, "Match number one, on the tee Mr Robert T Jones." The familiar plus-fours-clad figure strode forward and with that lovely, long, languid swing sent the ball sailing down the fairway to the crest of the hill. On his heels came Snead, the straw hat set at a jaunty angle. His drive flew long, but tailed away at the end and left him an awkward shot from the right across a sea of scrub. A large crowd followed the match as it progressed out into the country, but many stayed to witness the arrival of Hogan and Player. Hogan stepped forward on to the tee, coiled and cracked the ball arrow-straight. His face betrayed not an iota of emotion and Player, perhaps remembering the awe in which he held his opponent, rather hurried his tee shot and hooked it into the left-hand rough.

A burst of laughter greeted the next combatant – Hagen, acting out his philosophy of always stopping to smell the flowers by kissing a pretty girl and admiring the rose tucked in her buttonhole. Hagen was dressed in black-and-white brogue shoes, Argyll socks, cream plus-fours and a yellow sweater.

With barely a glance down the fairway, he lunged at the ball and sent it swinging away into the right-hand rough. Turning to the crowd, he said: "That stuff I was on last night didn't make me drunk, but I sure as hell fell down a lot." Even Palmer joined in the laughter for that one before he set down to the business of driving his tee shot far down the fairway, arms high in that familiar finishing flourish.

And finally the last two, Cotton and Nicklaus. Cotton looked taut, his face drawn, the shoulders sloped in the revealing left-to-right plane. He teed up and the hands moved through the shot and the ball fizzed from the tee as the striker reached that characteristic braced left-leg finishing position. Up stepped Nicklaus. With a massive wind-up he crashed the ball so far that it came to rest on the downslope of that 1st fairway, leaving its owner a nasty shot from an awkward stance.

Fortunes fluctuated wildly that first morning. Jones lunched abstemiously on a glass of milk and a sandwich, knowing that his one-hole lead over Snead would mean a supreme effort in the afternoon. Hogan stood five up on Player after 18 as the American had staged a near-repeat of his 1956 Canada Cup appearance on the same course and had played the first 10 holes in 35 strokes. Player, suffering from a vicious hook, repaired immediately to the practice ground. Hagen lunched on three Scotches to partner the three-hole deficit he was carrying against Palmer. Nicklaus and Cotton were all square, both having gone round in 68.

As the afternoon drew on it quickly became plain that Snead would not catch Jones as the amateur produced stroke after stroke of perfect weight and direction and when the match finished on the 15th green, Jones needed three fours for a 67. Player, meanwhile, was staging one of his renowned fight-backs and turned in 32 to wrest three of the five holes back. An eagle at the 12th by the South African put him only one down, but an imperious 3-iron by Hogan round the edge of the trees on the 15th gave the American a birdie putt which he holed to go back to two up.

They halved the 16th, and on the famous 17th Hogan struck two woods that sent the ball arching towards the green and Player's putt for a birdie slid by leaving him the vanquished and Hogan the victor.

Hagen, by dint of some remarkable recoveries, was still only two down as he and Palmer played the 13th and it was here that Hagen played the shot that was to break Palmer's heart. Cutting his second away to the right off that elusive green, Hagen found his ball buried in a clump of tall grass with a bunker between him and a pin that was set close to the right-hand side of the green. Forsaking all the usual preliminaries, Hagen thumped the ball out and it ran round the edge of the bunker, finally resting a few inches from the hole. A stunned Palmer three-putted to lose that hole. Another three putts at the next from the lower level and a hooked drive on 16 put him one down and, with Hagen making a wondrous four on the last from under the trees to the right of the green, Palmer was closed out by two holes.

The Nicklaus-Cotton saga saw the finest golf of that first day and both men came to the last all square. Two massive blows by the American saw him home in two and when his putt from fully 15 yards plunged into the hole. Cotton could only manage a wry grin as he walked forward to shake hands.

So the semi-finals were set between Jones and Hogan, artistry versus ice-cool precision, and Hagen versus Nicklaus, showmanship versus power. O.B. Keeler, Jones's close friend and reporter on all his man's great triumphs, felt that the Atlantan would be hard-pressed to sustain his energies for another 36 holes of gruelling combat. Hogan, on the other hand, was wrapped in that cocoon of concentration that had so impressed the Scots at Carnoustie 1953.

Jones swept away in the morning round striking woods smack into the heart of the greens and wielding Calamity Jane to deadly effect. Hogan's Achilles' heel, the short putt, proved his undoing on at least three holes and the man from Texas went into lunch four down. A tiring Jones was hauled back to only two up with three to play but a silky putt wafted across the 16th green and dropped to give the amateur a 3 & 2 win.

The other semi-final was really no contest. Hagen, who had booked a passage home on the QE2, seemed to have his mind fixed on the delights of life afloat and only some staunch recoveries kept the margin below the 12 & 11 defeat that Nicklaus inflicted upon him.

And so to a final that brought together the greatest of two eras if one used the criterion of major championships. Was there ever a match like it! A morning 66 by Nicklaus left him only one up as Jones produced a 67, the 17th, which Nicklaus eagled, being the only difference between them. The afternoon saw a freshening wind swirling through the trees and Jones, drawing on some hidden reserves of strength, flighted his shots low and true while Nicklaus watched some of his high-flying approaches catch the wind and swing away. Nicklaus putted phenomenally and was one down at the turn. They halved the next five, two of them with birdies, and stepped on to the 15th tee. Here Nicklaus unleashed a colossal drive that left him only a 4-iron into the green. When the shot squirmed to a halt only three feet from the hole, the match was all square. The 16th was halved in fours, the 17th in cagey fives and with the crowd almost beside itself, they marched to the last tee.

Jones's drive was long, low and possessed of that hint of fade that took it to the corner of the dog-leg. Nicklaus's drive was also long and also faded, but it was a fraction too high and the wind pushed it back so it came to rest 20 yards behind his opponent's. In a manner reminiscent of his drive to the 18th at St Andrews during the last round of the 1970 Open, Nicklaus took off his sweater and, drawing back his 3-wood, hit a stroke of such calculated power that those who saw it swear the ball gave an agonised cry. It was a stroke of sheer majesty and no one was surprised when the ball came to rest only 20 feet from the pin. How would Jones react? The answer was not long in coming. Jones too swung a 3-wood and the shot set off for the target as if held on line by an invisible hand. It pitched short of the green, skirted the bunker and ran up to lie 12 feet from the hole. It was an ecstatic moment as the two players walked through the cheering throng and then, as if orchestrated by an unseen conductor, the crowd fell silent as Nicklaus weighed up his putt. After what seemed an age, he struck it and the collective gasp from the spectators meant that it had just edged by. Now it was Jones's turn. He crouched behind his putt, brow furrowed in concentration, he stepped up and the soft sound Calamity Jane made signalled the start of the ball on its path. The ball curled down the gentle slope and...

It was now cold in the garret. The sun had long set but through the murky

shadows I could still see the blank sheet of paper staring back at me, defying me to mark its surface. The dream World Match-Play was over but I felt that somewhere in the recess of my mind lurked the germ of an idea. With eager fingers I began to type.
(1975)

FORA! FORA! FORA!

They came in low and fast that morning with the sun hard at their backs. Their track marks in the dew were the only indication of their arrival and before the Secretary had even unlocked the door to his office, they were in possession of the 1st tee, the pro's shop and the locker room.

Lifting his binoculars to his one good eye – he'd lost the other at West Hill – the Secretary saw that the task was almost beyond him. They'd moved too quickly and suddenly for him to mount anything but a futile gesture. Dragging his gammy leg, the result of a severed tendon from an earlier skirmish, he called Nigger, his faithful black labrador and limped to lock the door to the ladies' locker room. He knew it was a meaningless action at this stage but he was damned if he was going to let them completely overrun the club without showing some kind of spirit.

"Well, Nig, old boy," he said to the animal that looked up at him with large brown eyes, tail wagging furiously, "it looks like the end of the road for you and me but as long as there are men proud to call themselves British, as long as there's a flag to salute, then it's worth going on even if it means making the ultimate sacrifice." And the Secretary stumped off to meet the commander of the invasion force.

The Captain of the Micro-Widget Manufacturing Company Golfing Society was an honourable man. Educated at Oxford, he admired the British but felt them to be soft and in need of discipline. When the secretary entered the men's locker-room the Captain of the MWMCGS bowed deep and low. "Blitish Secletaly," he said, baring his teeth in an apology for a smile, "Blitish Secletaly will be preased to hand orer keys to erectic caddie cart shed." The enormity of this request was like a body blow to the Secretary but his face betrayed none of his emotions. "I am afraid," replied the Secretary, "that I cannot accede to your request."

"In rat case," said the Japanese Captain, "you reave me with no artelnative but to ret my men roose on your course. Prease to step outside where my men will show Impelial Japanese golfers do not take kindry to instluctions from Blitish pig dog Secletaly."

Outside was already a shambles – the greens staff had been herded into the gang mower shed, their engines silenced. The pro lay gibbering in the corner of his shop as one of the invaders read him the complete volumes of Isao Aoki's *Guide to the Oriental Golf Swing*, the sing-song tones acting as a refined form of water torture.

The steward had been forced into the kitchen where he had been ordered to prepare 50 meals comprising fresh bamboo shoots, long grain rice and chicken in soya sauce with saki to follow. The door to the electric caddie cart shed had been broken down and a squadron of carts, the Rising Sun flag fluttering from their bonnets, were patrolling the area round the 1st tee.

It was "Sailor" who was first to arrive. "Sailor", a veteran of Wentworth and the Old Course, a man who knew electric caddie cart strategy better than anyone. They still talked about him in the mess and how, in one dog-fight, piloting a Hurricane type cart with only two wheels and half his golf clubs gone, he's seen off six of the enemy. All they'd found of him afterwards was a leg and a piece of offal in the tee-peg compartment but Sir Archie had done a wonderful job of stitching him up and he was soon back in action.

This time he came at them head on, there was no time for cover or a subtle approach, he knew he had to hit and run and wear them down with the ferocity of his attack. Bearing down from the car park, and being a stickler for discipline, taking care to avoid the white lines indicating the area for the President's Rolls, he burst through the phalanx of Rising Sun flags. With a thrust of his new graphite-shafted brassie he took three of the enemy out on his first run, wheeled, and swiftly changing to a sand-wedge, removed two more on the return.

Confusion reigned in the Japanese ranks – they scattered, many of them belching flame from their engines, careering on a disaster course to plunge into the abyss that was the cross-bunker on the 1st fairway. Before they had time to regroup, "Sailor" was back, spitting defiance from his 1-iron with the grooved hosel and offset leading edge.

It was over almost as soon as it had begun. The tattered remnants of the MWMCGS, once a proud and arrogant body of men each committed to the five hour round and the keeping of every score, limped back to the clubhouse while the Secretary ran up the Union Jack on the club flag-pole. "I am prepared," said the Secretary, "to accept the unconditional surrender of your forces under the terms empowered to me by the Royal & Ancient Convention." The Japanese Captain once again bowed deep and low: "Prease," he said, "to accept folmal sullender but understand that for Japanese is no honour in defeat, onry shame." With that he drew his ceremonial putter and fell forwards on to the sharp end, uttering scarcely a moan as his blood tainted the velvet sward of the putting-green.

"Strange fellows," said the Secretary, looking down at his faithful black labrador and tapping his gammy leg with his wooden cane, "they used to do that when we saw them off the Burma Road."
(1986)

THE GOLFATHER

Joe "Hot Wedge" Bananas was angry. He stormed off the 18th green after his last round in the Lasagne Classic, having just three-putted the last six greens to throw away the first prize of 250,000 dollars and free spaghetti for life. He slumped in the locker room, his mind a confused jumble. "It's no good," he said, "I just can't putt. Only the Golfather can save me now."

Three hundred miles away in his heavily bunkered retreat the Golfather was holding court. Don Multio Paro was the Golfather. He had arrived in the country 40 years ago a nobody, a nothing pro hoping to scrape a living from the circuit. During those 40 years he had carved his reputation across the game to such an extent that his empire now extended from coast to coast. When a professional golfer anywhere holed a putt the Golfather knew about it and fast. Standing now in his living-room he looked an inconsequential figure until you noticed the steely blue of his grey-flecked eyes and the deference and homage those gathered around paid him.

The first supplicant shuffled forward. He was a small man wearing an old and rather shabby windcheater and waterproof trousers.

"Don Multio," he said, "it is I, your brother's sister's cousin's husband, who comes to see you about my daughter's hook."

"I remember you, my brother's sister's cousin's husband, and I know of your daughter's hook and how she came about it," replied the Golfather. "Those responsible have been taken care of, do not fear. But why, my brother's sister's cousin's husband, did you wait so long to come and see me? Why do you wait until you are in trouble before you visit your Golfather? Am I only to see you when things are not going right for you?"

The small man cringed.

"I am sorry, Don Multio, but I have been too busy with 20 lessons a day for the past two years, summer and winter. How else can a man like myself feed a wife and six bambinos?"

Don Multio looked at the small man with compassion; a thin smile crossed his lips.

"All right, my brother's sister's cousin's husband, go in peace, but one day I shall ask of you a favour and when I do you will remember this day."

"Yes, yes," replied the small man, "anything, Don Multio, you have only to ask and it shall be done."

With that the small man crept out gratefully from his audience with the Golfather, softly closing the door behind him. When the rustle of the small man's waterproof trousers had ceased in the passage outside, the Golfather turned to his lieutenants around him.

"No more audiences today, I am tired and my favourite Golfson is in trouble. That crazy boy 'Hot Wedge' has just three-putted the last six greens in the Lasagne Classic and he will be calling me shortly to arrange for me to get him in line. I need to concentrate, please leave me."

In another room of the Golfather's house, the telephone jangled.

Joe "Hot Wedge" Bananas was nervous. He sat outside the Golfather's study anxiously waiting the summons to enter and twisting his golf cap in his hands as he waited. The door to the study opened and one of the Golfather's hatchet men beckoned him in. The Golfather greeted his favourite Golfson affectionately.

"My son," he said, "how wonderful to see you." The Golfather stepped back. "But you do not look as you used to, you are a little flabby around the waist, your eyes are bloodshot, your hands shake. Why? What has happened to you?"

"It's my putting, Golfather," replied Joe, "for months I haven't holed anything over six inches, my nerves are shot to pieces. The only hope I have is to get hold of a new putter being made down in the South, but the guy won't let me have one because of my connections with you."

The Golfather looked angrily at Joe.

"It is not just the putter that is stopping you, my son, it is more. You have been watched and your movements checked, you have been leading a fine old life out there on the circuit, women, drinking, playing cards, going to bed late. You have behaved like a guinea-wop and now you ask me to help you. You are not worth helping."

"Please help me, Golfather, just this time," whimpered Joe, "I promise you that if you help me get this putter I will change my ways and get down to playing some serious golf on the tour, please help me and I promise you I'll be OK."

The Golfather motioned to one of his lieutenants. "Get this putter manufacturer on the phone and talk to him real nice about Joe here."

Joe clasped the Golfather by the hand. "You won't regret this, Golfather," said Joe, "but what are you going to say to the putter manufacturer?"

"Don't worry, Joe," said the Golfather, "we'll make him an offer he can't refuse."

The Chairman of the Southern Putter Manufacturing Company Inc. felt happy. He felt happy for two reasons. Firstly because he had put those guinea-wops in their place by refusing to supply them with a putter when they had phoned him earlier in the day. And secondly, because he had just locked up in his safe the thing that he prized most – his solid gold, centre-shafted putter with the mink grip. As the Chairman of the Southern Putter Manufacturing Company Inc. got ready for bed he whistled a little tune because he was happy.

During the night the Chairman of the Southern Putter Manufacturing Company Inc. woke up with the feeling that there was someone else in the room with him. He reached out for the light and as he did so his hand brushed against something soft and furry. He switched on the light, his panic rising, and threw back the bedclothes. There, broken in a hundred pieces, was his solid gold, centre-shafted putter with the mink grip. The Chairman of the Southern Putter Manufacturing Company Inc. opened his mouth in a long, agonising scream and his shrill ululations drowned the ringing of the telephone in the next room.

Seated in the basement of his house, the Golfather was speaking on the phone.

"I told you not to worry, Joe," he said, "we just made him an offer he couldn't refuse. Now you go out there and start winning again. That's OK, Joe, be a good boy so your Golfather can be proud of you."

The Golfather put the phone down, turned to his indoor putting green and sank another putt.

(1973)

BWANA GOLF

It was hot, He looked across the flat, baked African veldt and cursed the sun, the dust and flies. His hat, with "American Open Golf Championship" written across its front, was smeared with dirt and sweat.

"Christ!" he said, as he picked his teeth with a tee peg, "Why on earth didn't I stay on the nice easy American tournament circuit instead of coming out here?"

He leaned back in his mobile caddie-cart and reflected. He was 35 and at the zenith of his career. Leading money winner on the American tour, where he could drop a Santa Fe housewife in Bermuda shorts at 200 yards with a 3-iron or a Nassau businessman at 280 yards with a driver, he had the world at his spiked-shod feet. Then Grabber, his manager, had told him he would never be considered really great unless he went to Africa. So he had come.

That was two years ago, and here he was on his 50th safari, still searching for M'buru, the great elephant the natives called He-whose-tusks-are-thicker-than-Arnold-Palmer's-forearms. M'buru was an obsession, he must have him for himself to complete his Grand Slam. The Grand Slam consisted of a lion, a leopard, a rhino, a water buffalo and an elephant – he had bagged four of them but the elephant eluded him. Getting M'buru would give him the Grandest Slam of all.

That night they had pitched camp on the edge of a small donga (gully). Earlier, he had called for his chief caddie.

"Kidoko, come here you lazy nugu [ape] and bring my matched set of Scottish-made irons with the whippy shafts. I spy dinner out there."

Kidoko came running towards him, the big leather golf bag across his shoulders.

"Bwana," he said, a huge grin spreading across his dusky face, "is the Bwana going to shoot us some dinner?"

He looked at Kidoko with affection, the affection born out of two years of much laughter, a few tears and too many golf shots.

"Yes, Kidoko, I am going to shoot us some dinner."

About 100 yards away were a flock of guinea-fowl, quietly pecking at the arid earth. He selected a 4-iron, just right for a low trajectory and with enough power to do the job. He dropped half-a-dozen repainted Dunlops on the dusty ground and took a couple of practice swings. The guinea-fowl were still unaware of his presence when the first ball took the head off the leading bird. The others stood stock still for about 20 seconds, during which time three more shots found their mark. The remainder of the flock shot off at high speed and he ceased firing. The native caddies rushed out to the dead birds and cut their throats with swift strokes of their pangas (knives).

"Not bad, eh?" he said to Kidoko, "Four out of four."

"The Bwana is truly a wonderful player," replied Kidoko, "we will eat well tonight."

And Kidoko loped off to help prepare the fires. He felt good, those four shots had reminded him of the four kilted Scotsmen he had downed on the 16th at St Andrews when he had won his third Open Championship. He ate and slept well that night as the stars of the African sky twinkled like dew on the 1st green at Wentworth.

The messenger came at first light. He staggered into the camp, breathless and sweating.

"Bwana," he croaked, "I have seen him, not the length of Carnoustie from here, it is He-whose-tusks-are-thicker-than-Arnold-Palmer's-forearms as sure as God made little Gary Player."

A buzz of chatter rose from the natives and all eyes turned to the Bwana.

"Kidoko," he said quietly, "fetch my deep-faced driver with the stiff shaft."

Kidoko came forward bearing the beautifully balanced hand-made club, the best St Andrews could produce, and handed it to him. He felt the tacky leather grip in his hands and looked down the tempered steel shaft to the fine persimmon head – a feeling of almost sensual pleasure swept over him.

"This time," he thought, "this time I shall get you, M'buru." Then he walked over to the mobile caddie cart that Kidoko had already loaded with three dozen high compression Dunlop 65s and a gross of extra-long tee-pegs.

"We are ready, Bwana," said Kidoko.

"Right," he replied, "let's go!"

They drove for about half-an-hour in the direction the messenger had pointed out. They drove in silence over the rough terrain and when they were 500 yards from a clump of mopani trees, they saw him. It was M'buru. The great pachyderm was resting in the shade of the trees, his tusks stretching out in front of him, a cloud of flies forming a black halo above his wrinkled head. Kidoko stopped the cart and they alighted, keeping downwind from the clump of trees that shaded M'buru. Kidoko silently handed him the deep-faced driver and a fresh dozen balls and they crept towards M'buru. They stopped 200 yards from their quarry and he set up the dozen balls on the tee pegs.

He stepped back and checked his line, set himself up and, with a preliminary waggle, swung the club in that lovely rhythmic motion that was known from Sunningdale to San Francisco and hit it. He hit it with a hint of draw to bring it homing in on M'buru's head at the soft point below the ear, but as soon as the ball had left the club he knew the shot was wrong. It struck M'buru just above the leg in the hardened muscle of the shoulder and with a trumpeted scream of pain, five tons of enraged elephant lumbered to its feet, trunk extended, questing for this threat to its existence. The great ears flapped and M'buru faced his tormentors. Another block-busting drive caught M'buru in the chest.

"Too low," he muttered. M'buru pinned his ears back, folded his trunk under to expose the menace of his tusks and charged. One, two, three successive shots thudded into M'buru's skull and he stopped, shook his head as if to clear his brain, then he crashed to the ground, rolled over and lay still. Kidoko exhaled through flared nostrils.

"Bwana," he said, "today you have slain M'buru, the one we call He-whose-tusks-are-thicker-than-Arnold-Palmer's-forearms. You are indeed a mighty golfer and I salute you."

"I see you Kidoko," he replied, "and I salute you also. Let us go and examine the spoils of triumph."

When they reached the grey hulk that was once M'buru, the vultures were gathered in the surrounding trees, their hooked beaks sunk into the white collars of their necks.

"They look like greedy cousins waiting round a rich relative's death-bed," he said, "only this relative is dead and everything has been left to them."

He pegged a ball up and sent a shot clattering through the vulture-infested branches. They rose in clouds and circled wildly, squawking as they flew.

"Bloody aasvoles [vultures]," he said.

They had returned to the camp and sent the natives back to collect M'buru's tusks and cut up the carcass for fresh meat. It was a happy camp that night with much singing and drinking among them. Tomorrow he would have to begin the long trek back to the city and inform Grabber of his completion of the Grand Slam.

He was not looking forward to it. Two years was a long time to spend in one country and during that time he had grown to love Africa and its myriad faces. No doubt that greedy little swine Grabber would have another circuit lined up for him, probably something in the Amazon basin, hunting anacondas. He sifted the remains of his drink in his glass and threw them into the fire. It had been a long day.

Kidoko and the others watched him load up the caddie cart with his two sets of clubs. They watched him as he placed M'buru's tusks in the back and their hearts were heavy.

"We see you, Bwana," they chanted, "we see you are going and our hearts are heavy."

"I see you too," he replied, "and my heart is also heavy, but I must return to the city and catch the great silver bird that drops from the sky and seek the land of my forefathers. You must go to your kraals [huts] and service your wives and tend your cattle."

They watched him, Kidoko and the others, as he drove off and their chanting grew louder.

"Aiee!" they wailed, "Bwana Golf, we salute you."

"Bwana Golf," murmured Kidoko, "he was a man."

Soon, all they could see was a cloud of dust on the horizon and the rattle of his clubs was no more.

(1972)

IN WHICH CHRISTOPHER ROBIN DISCOVERS
A TREE THAT DISAPPEARS SOON AFTERWARDS

Christopher Robin knew all about trees. They were tall, green things and Owl lived in one, Piglet lived half-way down one and Pooh lived at the bottom of one only you didn't know it was Pooh's house unless you were Extremely Clever because above Pooh's house was a sign which said "Mr Saunders" which wasn't Pooh's name so unless you knew he lived there you wouldn't bother to knock if you were looking for him.

Christopher Robin also knew that Rabbit, Eeyore, Kanga, Roo and Tigger didn't live in trees but in other places, mostly under or on top of the ground. He tried to imagine Eeyore living on top of a tree but he couldn't because he knew that Eeyore liked thistles for breakfast and thistles always lived on the ground because otherwise you couldn't sit on them by accident. He had once seen Tigger up a tree with Roo but while Roo was jumping up and down on a branch singing "Look at me, I'm up a tree", Tigger looked Most Unhappy and Very Unbouncy and when Tigger came down he decided that Tiggers couldn't climb trees.

So you can tell that Christopher Robin knows all about trees.

Our story begins when Christopher Robin was out playing golf one day at a Rather Important Golf Club called Wentworth. He and Pooh had just returned from an Expotition to the North Pole where they had caught and tamed some Wild Woozles. Some of you may think that Christopher Robin and his friends only did things like going on Expotitions to the North Pole, rescuing Piglet from being entirely surrounded by water or looking for Heffalumps. But they did other things as well and one of them was playing golf. Christopher Robin liked playing golf because there were lots of trees around and he could carry on with his imaginings about whether Rabbit or Kanga could live up a tree.

Anyway, there was Christopher Robin playing golf and there were Pooh, Piglet, Tigger, Eeyore and Owl watching him. Pooh thought they had walked an awfully long way so he asked Christopher Robin how long the long way was and Christopher Robin had told him that when they finished they would have walked 18 holes.

And Pooh wondered how long that was and while he was wondering he thought of a little Wondering Hum which seemed a Good Hum to sing on a golf course.

I Wonder (by Pooh, a Bear)

I wonder why a golf course has 18 holes
I wonder why the world has the North and South Poles
I wonder why greenkeepers don't like moles
I wonder why a bear likes honey

Pooh was particularly proud of the last line because it reminded him that it was nearly time for a little smackerel of something and his tummy was thinking the same thing. But just as Pooh and Pooh's tummy were thinking the same thing, Christopher Robin said "Bother" in a very loud voice. Pooh and the others went over to see what it was that had made Christopher Robin say "Bother".

"What's happened?" said Pooh, seeing Christopher Robin looking sadly at the base of a tree.

"It would appear," said Owl, who knew a lot of long words, "that the projectile has come to rest in an unfavourable position."

"That's right, Owl," said Christopher Robin, "here's my ball almost in the middle of the 18th fairway and here's this tree surrounding it." And Christopher Robin said "Bother" again.

At the mention of the number 18 Pooh's tummy started being reminded again.

"Why not move the tree?" said Rabbit, who knew a lot about everything but not very much about golf.

"Why not move the ball?" said Eeyore in a gloomy voice. And that is what Christopher Robin did and then he stumped off muttering "Bother" just once more and the others followed him, all except Pooh.

Pooh didn't like to hear Christopher Robin say "Bother" and so he stayed behind to look at the tree. It wasn't much of a tree, thought Pooh, it wasn't very tall, it wasn't very green and it wasn't a tree that anybody could live on the top of, or half-way down or at the bottom. Tired out by his thinking, Pooh sat down and then, feeling more tired, leant against the tree. Being a Bear of short and stout proportions, the tree knew it was being leant against and being a tree of thin and ragged proportions, it didn't like being leant against. So it broke. And Pooh went tumbling backwards and the tree broke again. When Pooh got up, there were three very much shorter trees lying where only one tree once stood.

Pooh knew he was at a Rather Important Golf Club and was very worried about the tree he had made into three trees. Then he had a Brilliant Idea which, for a Bear of Very Little Brain, was a Brilliant Idea indeed. He picked up the three very much shorter trees and stuck them separately back into the ground in a sort of circle shape. "That," said Pooh to no-one in particular, "is much better." Then he walked off to tell Christopher Robin about his Brilliant Idea.

When Pooh found Christopher Robin he told him his Brilliant Idea so they all went back to look and Christopher Robin said that Pooh had been Exceedingly Clever to make one thin and ragged tree into three short and stout trees arranged in a sort of circle shape. They decided that Pooh's cleverness must be given a name and so Christopher Robin, who knew lots and lots of long words and could also spell, stood in the middle of the three short and stout trees and said: "I name these trees 'Christopher's Copse'," and then he said: "Otherwise known as 'Pooh's Plantation'." And Pooh felt very proud.

So the next time you play golf at that Rather Important Golf Club called Wentworth and on the 18th hole you see three trees grouped together just short of the green, you'll know why they are called Christopher's Copse otherwise known as Pooh's Plantation. It's because Christopher Robin knows all about trees and Pooh knows all about planting them.

With acknowledgement to Mr Eyre and Mr Methuen, publishers of those stories by that nice Mr Milne.
(1981)

TECHNOLOGICAL
REVOLUTION

RIP 1.62 INCHES

The death was announced on January 1st of Small Ball, who passed away peacefully after a legislative attack.

Born on May 1st, 1921 and weighing only 1.62 ounces, Small Ball became acknowledged as the ultimate influence in reducing scores and far superior to its ancestors, Featherie and Guttie. Small Ball's grandfather, Haskell Ball, known as "Big Coburn", had emigrated to America many years earlier but relations between the British and American sections of the family became increasingly strained.

In 1931, just before Small Ball reached his tenth birthday, the final split occurred when Big Ball was born on January 1st of that year in a small town in New Jersey. The birth was not an easy one with the issue weighing in at 1.55 ounces, but after a year Big Ball had grown to 1.62 ounces and to a height of 1.68 inches, 0.06 inches taller than his British counterpart. An uneasy truce then existed between the two with the American side of the family practising that well known isolationism that is still prevalent today by preventing Small Ball from visiting the States. On the other hand, the British penchant for fair play still prevailed and Big Ball was allowed over here without restriction.

The period between 1921 and 1931 was the golden age for Small Ball. Growing up in the Charleston era he was much sought after by the leading socialites of the day and spent many weeks criss-crossing the Atlantic in the company of such luminaries as Walter Hagen and Bobby Jones. Small Ball and Jones formed a particularly effective partnership and between them won 13 major championships in the period 1923-1930, the latter year being marked by victories in the British Amateur, the Open, the US Open and the US Amateur, known as the Grand Slam. Few people acknowledged the part

Small Ball had played in these triumphs as Jones himself was such a magnetic personality and captured most of the attention.

Following the final severance of relations in 1931, Small Ball settled permanently in England. Relieved of the pressures of trans-Atlantic travel he dominated the golf scene and from 1934, helped British golfers win the Open right up until the outbreak of World War II. His victory with Henry Cotton in 1934 earned him the accolade "Lord Dunlop of 65" and his elevation gave him the advantage over his great rival, A.E. Penfold of Birmingham. After the War, Lord Dunlop married the Countess of Slazenger and they had a son, the Earl of Warwick, and a daughter, Lady Spitfire. The dynasty appeared established but the first rumblings of discontent were heard in 1960 when a tournament was held at Wentworth in which Big Ball was compulsory. Four years later it was decreed that Big Ball would be used in all professional events but the Small Ball family, who had powerful friends in high places, managed to prevent this happening in 1965.

There was, however, no stopping the Americans with their brash ways and large amounts of money and in 1968 Big Ball took over the professional game for good despite an attempt to oust him in 1970.

By now the Small Ball fortunes were on the wane and the final death knell came in 1974 when Big Ball became the standard issue for the Open Championship. The Small Ball family retreated into a few reactionary enclaves throughout the country but by the dawning of the 1980s they were hardly ever seen. A few were sometimes discovered tucked away in the bottom of a locker or gathering cobwebs in someone's garage but very few, if any, were ever seen on a course.

There is no doubt that the arrival of Big Ball changed the face of British golf and enabled the top players to compete on equal terms with the Americans. Since this has been the case for the past decade it was decided that Small Ball had no relevance and when this news was released, Small Ball went into rapid decline, culminating in his death at one minute past midnight on January 1st, 1990, aged 68.

There are no surviving relatives and the funeral will take place in the R & A Museum.

(1990)

TIMELESS ANTIQUES ROADSHOW

The names of Bradbury Fisher and J Gladstone Bott do not exactly ring a bell in the folklore of golf. Not possessing any Scottish flavour, these two names fail to conjure visions of twilight on the 18th green at St Andrews, the cry of the curlew at Carnoustie or the strangled incantation of the visitor receiving his bill at Gleneagles.

Nevertheless, Fisher and Bott have their place in the game because when P G Wodehouse dreamed them up in a story he wrote called *High Stakes*, he made them both tainted American millionaires, hated rivals, somewhat eccentric players and avid collectors of golfing memorabilia.

Thus when Fisher had been prevented by his wife from purchasing J H Taylor's shirt stud, he was ripe for Bott's offer of the authentic baffy used by Bobby Jones in the Infants' All-In Championship of Atlanta in Georgia, open to those of both sexes not yet having finished teething.

Current collectors are no less dedicated in their search for items connected with golf that are antique, rare, or just plain unusual. The field is broad, covering old clubs and balls, books, trophies, pottery and china, ceramics and paintings and such has been the interest in recent years that collecting has become a growth industry.

The modern mass production of clubs and balls has led to a greater appreciation of the skills of the old club and ball makers who worked with crude implements to fashion the equipment of their era.

The golden age of club making was at the beginning of the 19th century. By and large, it was a family business operated by men who played the game professionally and augmented their income by manufacturing clubs. Almost all these firms stamped the company name on their products, so today collectors look out for names such as McEwan, Dunn, Patrick, Park, Morris, Forgan and Philp.

Philp, who was born near St Andrews in 1782 and became a club maker and repairer in 1812, has, in fact, become the Chippendale of golf club making.

When the gutta ball arrived in 1848, being a ball which didn't cut like a featherie, the use of iron clubs increased and club makers expanded their business to take in the work done by blacksmiths on the forging of iron heads.

Since clubs were hand made, no two were ever alike. The shafts would vary, as would the heads, and each club maker would have his own method of finishing off the product.

These old clubs are much prized by collectors and the auction houses have discovered there is a lucrative market among buyers from all over the world. It has now become part of the build-up to the Open Championship for the major companies to hold special golf memorabilia sales and in recent years prices have rocketed.

Last year, for example, a lady's rut iron, if you'll forgive the indelicacy, fetched over £500, and if you happen to own a featherie ball made by W & J Gourlay of Musselburgh then you are nursing a £3,000 item.

While the equipment is the glamorous side of golf collecting, there are rich pickings to be found in other memorabilia. The period between the wars produced a plethora of items including a complete Doulton dinner service with designs by Crombie – a noted golf artist – mechanical golfing toys, golf jewellery, postcards and silverware. Books on golf abound and certain limited editions fetch very high prices.

But let us not become too obsessed with the grubby commercialism of collecting. The game itself is often referred to as an art form so it is only natural that it should have created so much art and craft.

The true collector does not seize upon a rare item with the intention of turning over a fast buck, it is desirable for the quality of workmanship and its link with the past.

As a writer on the game, it is comforting to know that previous authors' works are so highly cherished. When my next book erupts from the typewriter, I exhort you to buy a copy. Who knows, in 50 years time you or your descendants could be the proud possessors of an extremely rare and valuable item which, as it appreciates, can also be used to prop up the rickety legs of the kitchen table.

(1986)

REDUCTION IN ARMS

Let us for a moment consider the number 14. There it is, tucked away in its correct place somewhere between ten and 20, and hardly anybody takes any notice of it.

But in golf that number has more relevance than in any other sports as, since 1938, it has been laid down as the maximum allowance for the number of clubs in each player's bag.

The figure was chosen arbitrarily to stop the trend at that time of professionals carrying a ridiculous amount of clubs for promotional purposes.

The leader in this activity was Walter Hagen, who carried as many as 28 clubs, no doubt contributing to him being able to live like a millionaire.

The question arises as to whether, after 50 years of intensive research by golfers throughout the world, 14 is the right number. Certainly there should be no more, so should there be fewer? Would fewer clubs make any difference to the general standard of play today?

The answer to that is an emphatic no. Furthermore, it is my contention that fewer clubs would actually improve general playing standards. As the game has progressed down its computerised path, the choice of clubs available has resulted in a standardisation of shot-making which has removed part of the game's challenge.

In professional golf that challenge barely exists. With swings honed by constant repetition on the practice ground and with yardage charts at the ready, today's tour player merely receives the information as to the distance of the shot in hand and then selects the club to cover that distance. He knows almost to the yard how far he hits with each club and simply uses the same swing for every shot.

Occasionally the game throws up a renegade such as Seve Ballesteros, who enjoys varying the swing and the type of shot. But, by and large, the professionals do not like to fiddle around; they want the security they have built for themselves on the practice ground.

In the 1975 US Masters, Johnny Miller, who ultimately finished second to Jack Nicklaus, complained after a first-round 75 that all his approach shots had been "in between clubs". In other words, unless he had precisely the right distance for a certain club he was flummoxed.

Such a situation would never occur with Ballesteros, who developed his game as a child on the beach at Pedrena with just a 3-iron. Nowadays youngsters start off with almost a full set. Far better for them to start out with just one club, say a 7-iron, and learn to play a variety of shots with that which they can adapt to the other clubs.

Golfers would become more skilful if the choice of clubs was limited so that they had to manufacture shots. Let us say, for example, that eight clubs became the limit. Therefore, the average bag would hold a driver, 4-wood, a putter and five irons of varying lofts.

This would put the challenge of the game right back where it belongs. It would also serve to make the game less expensive to take up, would do away with trolleys and speed up play as we walk around the course briskly carrying our lightweight bags. Dithering over club selection would also be reduced.

Now, as you are about to point out, there is nothing to stop you or me from carrying just eight clubs – 14 is only a maximum.

The trouble is that while that maximum exists, and human nature being what it is, we shall feel that whatever score we manage with eight clubs, we could have done better with the full quiver. Evidence provided by limited club competitions does not support this.

While legislation to reduce the maximum allowed is unlikely to be forthcoming, the opportunity to inject a little spice into the game is available.

How about a professional tournament with an eight-club limit on the players, no caddies and no yardage charts? And a two-shot penalty on any player who takes more than three hours to get round.
(1985)

What Did You Shoot?

It has been suggested that launching a projectile in the air represents man's deep-seated desire to fly and, if one looks back through history, there is ample evidence of this. Early man's flying instincts were nurtured by a more basic desire, namely the need to eat. When he discovered that it was easier to throw something at an animal rather than chase it, then he gradually evolved more suitable and powerful means of doing the throwing.

Probably the most effective of these early weapons was the bow and arrow and, when archery became popularised by the result of Agincourt, then man, whether he knew it or not, was well on the way to inventing golf.

There is much in common between the two activities. Both require the launching of a missile at a distant target, both are conducted in the open and are thus subject to the vagaries of the weather, both use implements constructed of wood and metal, and both require co-ordination if the shot is to be launched successfully.

If it were possible to step back in time, I'm sure we would find that the archers of yesteryear had a very similar attitude to today's golfers. To begin with there would be much discussion on technique, the straight left arm would have been mandatory (left handers please reverse instructions) as would the need to keep the head still.

The width of the stance would have been subject to many variations and no doubt controversy would have raged over the grip on the bow, the position of the right elbow and the distance the arm should be drawn back while still retaining control.

The leading marksmen (markswomen would have been excluded) would pass among the lesser lights imparting words of wisdom and, at the end of the day, as they quaffed their mead, the archers would exchange stories of arrows that fell short, accidentally struck a passer-by or were successful. Maybe archers were the first people to use the expression "What did you shoot?"

The connection would have been maintained in the area of equipment. The archers would be plugging away with the standard bow of yew and then someone would come along with one made of say, larch. The archers would gather round: "Too whippy" one would say, "No feel" would say another, while a third would find it was exactly right and gave his arrows another 20 yards in flight. The arrival of the steel bow was probably as momentous as that of the steel shaft and now bows are made from modern materials like fibreglass and carbon fibre.

The arrow itself could be likened to the golf ball and although the only arrow I have ever released flew exactly where I knew it would, *viz*: high and right, no doubt technology has enabled the archer to have available arrows suitable for varying wind conditions and temperature extremes.

Whether the archery industry has reached the limits of technological advance I do not know, but that is certainly not the case in golf. The changes are all around us from frequency matched shafts and the paradoxically named metal woods right through to coloured golf balls.

There is no doubt that the governing bodies are worried about these improvements by club and ball, fearing that they could prove detrimental to the basic challenge of the game. If new equipment reduces that challenge then the enjoyment is also reduced.

Although there is a velocity restriction on the golf balls it is apparent from the constant lengthening of courses that the assistance modern equipment provides is responsible for this disturbing trend. Any golfer who has struck a two-piece ball as opposed to a wound ball will know the difference in the feel of the shot and before too long will also know that the two piece appears to run further on landing. When the golfer is armed with a metal wood and a two-piece ball then the potential for greater length is vastly increased.

Admittedly the average golfer is still faced with the possibility that this equipment may propel the ball even further off line but in the hands of an accomplished player, great courses and superbly structured holes are at risk.

The metal wood is now established as a legitimate weapon in the quest for power and as the two-piece ball has grown in popularity it may become the only practical club to use as conventional woods can be damaged by two-piece balls.

On the subject of coloured balls I am less ambivalent. I think they are a monstrous innovation, a garish vulgarity that would be better located in a fairground shooting gallery. So far as I'm concerned there is only one place for coloured balls and the whereabouts of them is hardly suitable fare for a family newspaper.

In my nightmare I see serried ranks of professionals loosening up on the practice ground, their metal woods glinting in the sun as balls of various hues disappear into the distance, like star shells.

The collective noise they make reverberates around the arena as they prepare to tackle a layout which covers roughly the same area as the Brazilian rainforest, measured in metres, of course.

Meanwhile out on the course, the tee markers are indicated by the presence of two performing seals, each with a coloured golf ball perched on the end of its nose.

(1990)

THE HASKELL LETTERS

In 1892, Coburn Haskell moved from his home town of Boston to Cleveland to join his colleague, Bertram Work, in developing a rubber-wound golf ball. It took them six years before their idea of wrapping thin rubber strips round a central core under tension was finally accepted by the US Patents' Office.

Like many good ideas, Haskell's new golf ball was not immediately recognised and faced opposition from several quarters, not least Haskell's own parents, whose role in the affair has remained unrevealed until the discovery of a bundle of old letters.

• • • • • • •

Cleveland, Ohio
February, 1892

Dear Mom and Pop,

Just a quick note to let you know how I'm getting on. The weather has been appalling and my little research laboratory is colder than a husky's backside but Bertram and I are close to a breakthrough.

You remember I told you about Bertram in one of my earlier letters and you wrote back that Bertram Work sure sounded a funny name for a guy who sits around all day measuring the co-efficient of elasticised rubber in relation to the amount of tension exerted. Since then, Bertram and I have come up with the goods and we're hoping to register our idea with the Patents' Office.

I hope you are both well and could you please send me another $20 to tide me over.

Your affectionate son,
Coburn

• • • • • • •

Boston, Massachusetts
March, 1892

Dear Coburn,

Thank you for your letter. Your father and I are extremely worried about you and your apparent obsession with rubber. We thought we had told you about the things normal people did when we found you playing "Doctors and Nurses" with little Rose May behind the woodshed.

Now you are a grown man and you appear to be not only some kind of rubber fetishist but you are also spending all your waking hours with this other man.

Where did we go wrong, Coburn? Your father and I are ashamed to talk about you to our friends and your grandfather, Henry Cabot Haskell, is thinking of cutting you out of his will.

I shudder to think what you are taking down to the Patents' Office and pray that whatever it is, you won't put your name to it – we Haskells have a reputation to consider.

I am enclosing $20 in the hope that you will use it to catch a train back to Boston and then book into a clinic. I have been reading about this Austrian, Sigmund Freud, in the newspapers and a visit to him could help solve your problems.

Rose May has been seen out walking with one of the Kennedy boys, so please take my advice before it's too late.

Your loving mother

• • • • • •

Cleveland, Ohio
April, 1892

Dear Mom and Pop,

Many thanks for your letter and the $20. Things are looking much better now. The patent for the new ball should be through soon and we can start production.

I took some prototypes along to the Country Club here and was able to reach the 380 yard 1st hole with a drive and a mashie. With the old gutty I've always needed two wooden club shots. Bertram and I are really excited and once the royalties start coming in, the future is secure.

Who is this guy Freud? Does he know anything about dimple configuration? I am not particularly worried about Rose May walking out with one of the Kennedy boys, they are only Irish-American and "new" money and the family will never amount to much.

Your devoted son,
Coburn

● ● ● ● ● ● ●

Boston, Massachusetts
May, 1892

Dear Coburn,

We are in receipt of your last letter. Frankly Coburn, your father and I are in despair. When you left for Cleveland we thought you would find a nice, safe job as a chemist but since you've fallen in with that dreadful man, there appears little hope of that.

How on earth can you secure your future by developing a new golf ball? Your father and I know very little about the game but your grandfather, Henry Cabot Haskell, is a pillar at the Country Club at Brookline and when we told him about your new ball he said it would never catch on. He is still considering cutting you out of his will. Please come home so we can talk this thing through.

I saw Rose May the other day and she said that the Kennedy boy, Joseph I think his name is, is probably going to propose. If you came home, I'm sure you two could get together again.

Hopefully,
Your loving mother
(1984)

ONE BORN EVERY MINUTE

How is your golf at the moment? Still slicing those drives, topping those iron shots, fluffing those chips, and missing those short putts?

Well, take heart, for whatever particular affliction ails your game, some enterprising golf equipment manufacturer has come up with an amazing new and revolutionary piece of advanced technology, which will transform your game from the depths of inadequacy to the heights of perfection.

Research into what makes golfers tick must have revealed that they are among the most gullible sportsmen and women. There can be no other reason for some of the preposterous claims put forward by the manufacturers to promote their products.

One only has to study some of the advertisements in the golf magazines to realise that golf equipment has come a long way since the days of hickory shafts. But what the golfers of yesteryear would make of such expressions as "penetration weighting", "frequency matched" or "kick zone", can only be imagined.

These expressions, and others like them, are part of today's technical jargon which is aimed at luring golfers into believing that they can buy a better game off the shelf.

The dominant theme in all this promotion is distance. Of all the strokes available to golfers, the one that guarantees universal satisfaction is the mighty tee shot which flies straight and true down the fairway, coming to rest some 300 yards from the tee.

Practically every club and ball manufacturer claims that: (a) his clubs hit the ball further, and (b) his ball flies further. These claims are not restricted to just these parts of the armoury. Manufacturers of shoes, golf gloves, shirts and tee-pegs have all jumped on the long driving bandwagon to the extent that were a player able to combine all these length-increasing gimmicks into one shot, the ball could be driven over 500 yards.

Knowing that length isn't everything, I regard these various claims with a great deal of circumspection. What I'm looking for is help in lowering my score and a glance through some recent American golf magazines has provided the answer.

First of all there are the grips on your clubs. According to Ken Venturi, the 1964 US Open champion, if you fit the grip that he endorses, you will lower your scores by three to four strokes a round. So if, like me, you score in the mid to low 80s, you are already down to the high 70s.

Dramatic progress is guaranteed by the Minus Ten Golf Link Company of San Jose, who promise to take 10 strokes off my score if I send them $7.95 for a transfer to stick on my driver, bearing the message "Stay Down". Although I'm not certain of its legality in actual play, I'm prepared to risk it, now that I'm scoring comfortably in the high 60s.

My next acquisition is going to render previous scoring records obsolete. This is the Controller Driving Iron, which automatically corrects hooks and slices, hits the balls 30 to 50 yards longer, and is absolutely guaranteed to lower your scores by five to 10 strokes.

I don't wish to appear greedy, so I'll take an eight-stroke reduction, and I've already rushed $89 to the National Golf Centre of Connecticut. I'm confident that this financial outlay will be handsomely recouped in winning bets from people who haven't taken advantage of these amazing offers.

Finally, and here I am in danger of making the game ridiculous, if I order a new super ball that flies like a U-2 airplane, putts with the steady roll of a cue ball, and bites on the green like a dropped cat, I will cut my scores by a further five to 10 strokes. This ball is on offer from the same people who are sending me the Controller, so if I send them $109 for the balls, perhaps I'll get a discount for bulk ordering.

You can see that by avoiding the outlandish claims for more distance and instead concentrating on stroke-saving ideas, I am about to score consistently in the mid-50s for a modest outlay of £150.

What do you mean there's one born every minute?

(1992)

JACOBS' CRACKER

If you are among the great majority of golfers who watch in anguish as your tee shots travel 100 yards up the fairway before veering alarmingly to the right to cover the next 100 yards in a sideways fashion, be assured that somebody has been thinking of you.

That somebody is John Jacobs, generally acknowledged as Britain's best golf teacher and a man whose career in this field has brought him into contact with thousands of different golfers. "At least 75 per cent of the golfers I teach," says Jacobs, "slice the ball with the longer clubs and pull the ball with the short irons. This is because they hit the ball with an out-to-in swing and with the club face open at impact."

Realising that golfers afflicted with these ailments find it difficult to actually change their swings, Jacobs set about designing a set of clubs in conjunction with Dunlop which would help reduce the slicing/pulling syndrome without the golfer having to change his natural swing.

At this stage it may help to have a PhD in ballistics for the way a golf ball reacts off the face of the club is the key factor in the design of the new clubs. Jacobs contends that basically the variations that occur in the flight of the golf ball derive entirely from the varying degrees of loft each club possesses. Therefore, the driver and the straighter-faced iron clubs strike the ball much higher up on its equator and the higher that point of impact is, the more sidespin is applied to it.

This is the sole reason why golfers find it easier to hit a 4-wood than a driver because the greater loft on the four wood enables the player to make contact with the ball lower down and impart underspin instead of sidespin. The greater the loft on a club the more underspin is applied so when a golfer with an out-to-in swing uses a short iron with its greater loft, the ball continues in its starting direction – pulled to the left.

The macho instinct that lurks inside every male golfer usually prevents him from taking a 4-wood from the tee in the interests of keeping the ball in play – he persists in using his driver because he is worried about losing distance. Perceptive readers will have already come to the conclusion that the way to counteract this approach is to produce a driver with more loft, thereby satisfying the psychological lust for power but at the same time providing a little more control.

This is what Jacobs has done to his woods but he has added one or two refinements. Since the greater loft would tend to give the ball a higher trajectory, the clubs are top weighted to counteract this; secondly, the faces of the clubs are slightly closed and the signature on the top of the heads is angled slightly inside the target line to encourage an inside takeaway on the backswing.

Similar refinements have been made on the iron clubs with the longer irons being given a more upright lie, which helps the golfer close the face at impact, and all the irons have a higher toe than usual which has the same effect as top-weighting the woods. Finally, both woods and irons have thinner grips and lighter swing-weights to promote clubhead speed.

For many years golf club manufacturers have been extolling the virtues of their wares, sometimes making the most preposterous claims for their equipment. The theory behind the Jacobs clubs certainly seems soundly based, although critics in the professional ranks have been quick to point out that the clubs are pandering to a swing fault when the real salvation lies in altering that swing.

Jacobs accepts that his clubs are of little value to the minority of the golfing population who hook the ball, but his experience is that no matter what they are told to do to alter their swings, golfers will revert to what feels natural to them. Frequency of lessons is another factor to be considered as most golfers do not have the time or the inclination or, indeed, the money, to embark on a protracted run of lessons to rebuild their game totally.

Since the slice is the dominant fault among golfers, anything that can assist in reducing that fault must have a fair chance of success. It has to be said, however, that no club is ever likely to be designed to prevent golfers from perpetrating the myriad of horrible shots that are at their disposal.

As one golf writing colleague said after nine holes with the new clubs: "What I want Jacobs to do next is design a club that will make me give up this bloody game altogether."
(1981)

PUTTING ON THE AGONY

THE LONG AND SHORT OF PUTTING SALVATION

Peter Senior's victory in the European Open put the finishing touch on one of the most remarkable comebacks in the game. At the beginning of last year, Senior was on the verge of giving up golf to concentrate on his pawnbroking business back home in Australia.

Such was Senior's mental state that it was doubtful whether he could have hit any of the three balls hanging outside his business premises. He had one of the most serious cases of the yips that anyone had ever seen and latterly was attacked by an inability to complete a full swing of the club. He would take the club back and then remain locked, unable to finish the stroke.

His putting salvation came in the form of a 48 inch weapon of the kind used by Sam Torrance. Senior tried it out and embarked on the same rehabilitation programme as Torrance had used when he had also found himself incapable of holing putts using a conventional putter.

Within months Senior was a changed man and at the end of last year completed a hat-trick of victories by winning the Australian PGA, the Australian Open and the Johnnie Walker Classic, the last being achieved at Royal Melbourne, whose greens are regarded as some of the fastest anywhere. Now he had become the first player to win in Europe using a putter that could equally serve as a crutch.

No other department of the game has been subject to such eccentric club design as putting. Ever since Walter Travis won the 1904 Amateur Championship at Sandwich using the Schenectady putter, the forerunner of the centre-shafted model, the administrators have looked askance at unusual innovations.

As the study of putting became more scientific it was clear that the ideal movement should be based on a pendulum stroke.

Putting in a conventional manner cannot achieve this since the right hand is lower than the left on the grip. The only way the human frame can create a true pendulum movement is for the putter to be swung back between the legs croquet fashion. This idea was hit upon more than 30 years ago by an inventor named Gillespie who came up with a T-square putter about two feet long. This enabled the user to place both hands together level on the grip and by swinging back between the legs it was impossible to twitch. Gillespie actually insured for £1,000 against his putter being banned and within a few months cashed in.

Sam Snead was the first player of note to putt croquet style using an extra long putter but then the authorities pulled a flanker by introducing a rule which prevented a player hitting a shot with the feet straddling the line. Snead simply circumvented this by standing to one side of the ball. Other players of Snead's generation have found a new lease of life on the American Senior Tour with the crutch putter although people like Arnold Palmer have resisted using it since they feel it just doesn't look right.

Wilson, the manufacturers of the Senior and Torrance model, assure me that sales of the putter are soaring. However, I haven't seen many club golfers using them, probably because they don't want to invite any more ridicule than the game usually inspires.

For Senior and Torrance the crutch putter means money in the bank. The rest of us may take a little longer in persuading. Even the diehard traditionalists might be tempted if it would guarantee that they would never again miss one of "those".
(1990)

Venom That Poisons the Putting Game

Those of you familiar with the tale of Rikki Tikki Tavi will know that it concerns the decimation of a family of cobras by the eponymous mongoose of the story.

The reason I mention it in the context of golf is that just recently there has been a strange transformation of my putting, whereby the putter has assumed the role of the live snake and the hole has become the mongoose.

My putter sits in the bag as a solid, dependable piece of metal, but as soon as I take it out it undergoes a metamorphosis. From 20 feet or so the putter retains its solidity, but as I get nearer the hole I find I am holding the tail of a three-foot long cobra which is about to plunge its fangs into my left ankle.

Worse still, when the ball and hole are both in my vision, the hole takes on the guise of a mongoose ready to spring. Since these two creatures are doing their level best to avoid each other, the ball becomes a mere plaything to be shuffled back and forth between the two.

Psychiatrists would have a field day with this one. However, a psychiatrist who played golf would simply shut his notebook, put a consoling arm around my shoulder and say: "Sorry old chap, there's nothing I can do. You've got 'em."

What he would be referring to are commonly known as the yips, that involuntary spasm which occurs when a golfer finds himself incapable of holing out from anywhere over six inches.

Countless theories have been put forward as to why the yips strike some players and not others. In assessing this malaise, it struck me that all the discussion on the subject is confined to males. I cannot recall ever hearing of or reading about or actually seeing a top-class woman golfer afflicted with the twitch.

Why should this be so? Why should the yips, like prostate glands and haemophilia, be a purely male affliction? It is often said that women golfers make up for their lack of power by possessing superb short games, but this is a fallacy.

The short game is one area where it is feasible to make comparisons between the sexes since sheer physical strength is not a factor. Yet, speaking as an unashamed admirer of women's golf, male golfers at the highest level have a superior short game. Herein may lie the root cause of the dreadfuls on the green. Man is by nature the hunter, the provider and the aggressor – not only is he designed for this purpose, society expects him to fulfil this role.

When he is pursuing his role in the competitive strata of his occupation then his aggression is at its strongest. Thus, when he is making his living from playing the game, his aggression is channelled into hitting the ball as close to the hole as possible and then, aggressively, going for the putt.

When women professional golfers are competing with each other, their natural instincts prevent them from being over-aggressive and, although they are trying to hit the ball close to the hole and make the putt, they do not attack with the same conviction as men.

While the male ego demands that a man has to prove he is superior to his fellows, women have no such problem. Male golfers at all levels believe that the game is all about macho war substitute stuff and hitting the ball miles from the tee. The small act of putting is almost akin to a fairy's pastime, it diminishes the masculinity.

Professional golfers realise the importance of putting and spend hours working on it. But when the putting goes it is because the macho instincts have betrayed them.

Women do not see the game as comprising two separate games. Putting is as much a part of the game as anything else and there's nothing demeaning about rolling the ball along the ground. This balanced approach is, to my way of thinking, the reason why women golfers do not contract the yips. (1991)

TIME WILL REMEMBER THE PLIGHT OF CORNISH SURVIVORS

Survivors from the good ship St Mellion will have a story to tell their grandchildren when they recount the events of this year's Benson and Hedges International Open. Trouble is, there were not that many survivors because this was more like an expedition to the South Pole rather than a trip to the south west.

First loss amid the Cornish tundra was Ian Woosnam, swept away by the icy winds and a severe attack of PMT (Post-Masters Travail). This ailment also afflicted Nick Faldo and to a lesser extent Sandy Lyle, and I don't suppose there has ever been an occasion when the last three Masters champions have all failed to break 80 in the same round, as was the case on the second day.

Even the scoreboard had a flavour of ice skating about it as eights and nines abounded, interspersed by the odd imperfect 10.

One can only feel sympathy for the sponsors who, on the 21st anniversary of their tournament, found an over-crowded TV schedule forcing them to accept such an early date. Next year we shall be back again in May and maybe this time the course will play as it was designed.

There is always one student who has revised more thoroughly than the rest. There was no Masters let down for Bernhard Langer, whose second round of 68 at the height of the gale was nothing short of miraculous and whose homeward 32 in the final round represented golf of the highest class.

One does not play 27 holes in the vilest of conditions in 100 strokes unless the putter is doing its stuff and, in this respect, I believe Langer has a distinct advantage. His putting woes of the past have been well chronicled and he has now devised the somewhat eccentric style of gripping the putter with the left hand only and then clamping the grip to his left forearm with his right hand.

This means that Langer has only one hand actually touching the grip and, while conventional putters were trying to maintain some feel and touch in their hands, he had no such problems.

In cold and windy conditions the paradox arises in that the hardest part of the game is not controlling the ball in the air, when it is prey to the elements, but when it is on the ground. Part of the problem is that you are not making any big movement and your body should remain still.

Then you have to make yourself hit the ball hard enough on a downhill putt with the wind against and not too hard on an uphill putt with the wind behind.

Cross-wind putts with the borrow going the opposite way are equally nightmarish so the whole process becomes rather like rubbing the top of your head and your stomach in different directions at the same time.

The professionals take steps to combat the wind by widening their stance and crouching down lower over the ball to reduce their exposure.

Players such as Sam Torrance and Peter Senior, who both use the broom handle putter, still have to stand tall to the ball which makes Torrance's victory in the gales of the Jersey Open all the more remarkable.

Talking of the long putter, I'm still not convinced it conforms to the traditional style and design of a club. There are strong rumours that the governing bodies aren't convinced, either, but are loath to ban them in case they stir up a hornet's nest of litigation.

Steps have already been taken to ban the split grip on these putters and it may be that there will be a ruling stipulating the length of shaft allowed. Another suggestion is that a rule is introduced whereby the shaft of the putter may not touch any part of the body other than the hands and arms, thereby preventing the player from holding it under his chin or against his chest.

Apart from the US Senior Tour, where it is practically *de rigueur*, and a handful of touring professionals, the broom handle putter has failed to sweep through the amateur ranks.

As long as man continues to explore the finite part of putting he will always hope the equipment will gain him an extra edge. In the end, though, it is not the brains that go into the making of the club, it is the brains in the person holding it.

(1991)

BEAUTY ONLY SKIN DEEP

Towards the end of last year I celebrated a 25-year relationship with my putter. We didn't mark this anniversary in any particular style, just a quiet potter round the putting-green and a few reminiscences about the old days.

I remember clearly the day we first met and over the years my putter has demonstrated many quirks and foibles which imbued it with female characteristics. However, there has never been anything chauvinistic in my treatment of her. I have always regarded her as an equal in most respects and superior in other. I've even taken her into the Royal & Ancient clubhouse!

But, as in many relationships which last this long, there comes a time when the old sparkle is just not there. No more do we skip gaily through the grass in search of fresh greens to conquer and, instead of spending hours on the practice green, there is a distinct inclination on her part to stay in the bag with the rest of the clubs.

This deterioration did not happen overnight, there was no dramatic bust-up; indeed, we've hardly ever had a cross word. We just drifted into that rather dull acceptance of each other's idiosyncrasies.

The rot set in when a friend took her out of the bag one day and declared that she was illegal. The face that had sunk a thousand putts had become so worn away that she stood in the dock, condemned under Rule 4.1e, which says that the face shall not have any degree of concavity.

I was horror-struck that we had been playing, and occasionally winning, in sin. There were mitigating factors under Rule 4. I.f, which covers wear through normal use, but I decided that drastic action was required – an appointment with the local plastic surgeon at my club.

The prognosis was encouraging. "No problem," said the professional. "I'll soon have her looking 20 years younger. She could do with a new grip as well. Call back in a couple of days."

When I collected her she certainly looked better, the new grip fitted her perfectly and her face was gleaming. But, although her features were now finely chiselled, they had that taut, stretched look that one usually associates with ageing Hollywood film stars.

Would she, I wondered, as I took her out on to the putting-green, rekindle that desire which so enraptured me all those years ago? My first tentative strokes confirmed my worst fears. She may have looked better but the attempt to reverse the ravages of time had left her sullen and lifeless. The silky touch I had grown to love was no longer there – beauty was only skin deep.

I broke it to her gently for I am a compassionate man. I explained that I wasn't forsaking her for a younger more vivacious partner and that she would always have a cherished place in, if not my heart, then certainly the corner of my office. She took it remarkably well. There were no tantrums, no tears, no threats of a palimony suit. Secretly, I think she was quite relieved not to have to continue the charade.

Her replacement is of the younger more brash generation. A sort of break-dancing, finger-snapping, go-go putter. But boy, can she do the business. Once she gets out there she can't wait to get on with it. Insatiable would be an apt description, and at my age...

As for my old flame? Occasionally I give her a run on the carpet and, who knows, if the break-dancer burns herself out she may be called out of retirement.

(1983)

WHO'S WHO

ARNOLD PALMER

Some moments are forever etched into the memory, moments that the passing of time cannot diminish nor age dispel, and in their recalling they are as vivid as they were at the time of their passing.

One such moment occurred on a glorious October day 15 years ago when Wentworth was clad in its most splendid autumn colours. It was the semi-final of the then new Piccadilly World Match-Play Championship and the beginning of the afternoon round of the match between Arnold Palmer and Gary Player. The details of the morning round are somewhat hazy but on the 1st hole of the afternoon, Palmer provided me with that moment which is branded in my mind.

His drive had finished in the right-hand rough leaving him a perilous line for the second shot across scrub and the right-hand greenside bunker. He selected what looked like a 4-iron and with that quick, lunging swing, hit the ball with a ferocity I have never seen since.

I can see the flight of the ball even now, arching over the attendant trouble like a tracer-bullet and finally squirming to a halt some eight feet from the flag. The putt was a formality and so, as it turned out, was the match, for Palmer played the first six holes that afternoon in 19 strokes, and poor Player was buried under the onslaught.

Moments like that were part of the Palmer legend, for no other player had captured the imagination of the public in such a compelling manner. That stroke he hit at Wentworth could just as easily have shot out to the right to finish in the undergrowth but it probably wouldn't have mattered if it had for he would still have made the impossible recovery and holed the putt. The calculated risk was never part of Arnold Palmer's game, for calculating the possible results of a poor shot meant admitting the shot couldn't be played. That kind of thinking never entered his head – the ball was there to be hit and hit hard, and when it arrived on the green, it had only one destination.

There comes a time in any field of endeavour when a man emerges who is a notch above his contemporaries, who sets a standard the others are forced to follow and in so doing they find their performance rising above its normal level. Arnold Palmer was such a man. He was the right man at the right time, for his appearance coincided with rapid growth of the game, or maybe, it was he who was responsible for that growth. Either way, Palmer became the symbol of professional golf, not only through the dynamism of his play but also in the projection of his personality. The public could identify with Palmer like no other player before him. He was one of them and they could relate to his game for they too hit it into the trees and they too sometimes effected the astonishing recovery.

Such a folk-hero attracted an enormous following and Palmer rarely let them down. They also made him a very rich man, the first of golf's millionaires, and through Mark McCormack, Palmer's name was marketed in such a way that he was probably the most famous athlete in the world.

There is no doubt that British golf and the Open Championship in particular benefited from Palmer's influence, for it was he who gave that event the international status it enjoys today. When Palmer first came to Britain in 1960 he was the current US Masters and US Open champion, both victories having been achieved in typical Palmer fashion. At Augusta in April he had birdied the final three holes to win by a stroke from Ken Venturi, and at Cherry Hills in June, he produced a final round of 65 to make up seven strokes on the third round leader and win by two.

Palmer came to St Andrews for the Centenary Open eager to emulate Hogan, who arrived at Carnoustie in 1953 with the same two titles already won. He failed narrowly, losing by a stroke to Kel Nagle, but vowed to return until he had won. The following year he did win, pounding the ball low through the wind and rain at Royal Birkdale and gathering a whole new attachment of recruits to his army in the process. In the spring of the following year, Palmer won the Masters for the third time, defeating Gary Player and Dow Finsterwald.

Of his three US Open play-offs the one which scarred him the most was in 1966 at Olympic in San Francisco. With rounds of 71-66-70 and with an outward 32 in the final round, Palmer held a seven stroke lead over his nearest pursuer, Billy Casper, with whom he was playing. Many words have been written in an attempt to analyse how Palmer lost all those seven strokes in nine holes and ultimately the play-off, but the essence of that loss was the essence of Palmer himself. Here was a man playing with another whose approach to the game was the very antithesis of his own. Casper was a nudger, a straight-up-the-middle-into-the-best-position player who took no risks and relied on a lovely putting touch. There was Palmer, all fire and aggression, going for the big carry, hitting the ball, finding it and hitting it again.

On the 16th tee of that fateful last round Palmer's lead was down to three strokes and it was here he became a victim of his own image. The hole was a par five, dog-legging to the left, ideally suited for a drive with draw. Palmer knew he could hit a couple of 1-iron shots short of the green, pitch up and take a safe par, but he knew that wasn't his style. Furthermore, he knew it wasn't the style the public expected of him. He went for the controlled hook with a driver, pulled the shot into the trees and took six. Casper played the lay-up game, pitched on and holed the putt, did the same on the next hole, a long par four where Palmer again found trouble with a hooked tee shot, and the championship was tied.

Palmer's loss of that title was every bit as dramatic as his winning of others, but there is no doubt in my mind it affected him deeply in much the same way as Doug Sanders' missed putt in the 1970 Open, or Tony Jacklin's loss of the 1972 Open affected them. Such shattering defeats take their toll, leaving the recipient with that haunting doubt as to what might have been. It says much for Palmer's courage that he came back and continued to win tournaments, even to threaten for another US Open title in 1972 when he finished fourth.

In June 1962 he lost a play-off to Jack Nicklaus for the US Open at Oakmont, and arrived at Troon for the Open Championship to find a course baked hard by the summer sun and unpredictable in its bounce.

To many of the players, Troon appeared unplayable and quite a few of them said so. Whatever Palmer thought about the course, he kept his feelings to himself and produced what many observers felt was the finest golf of his career in winning the title by six strokes from Nagle and by 13 from the third placed man. He also set a new Championship record of 276 which stood for 15 years, although it was equalled by Tom Weiskopf round the same course in 1973.

That was to be his last Open victory, but not his last major championship win; in 1964 he decimated the field in the Masters to take his fourth green jacket by six strokes. His total of seven major championship victories may look meagre compared with Nicklaus' 15, but it should be remembered that he lost three play-offs for the US Open title, proof that he could handle the demanding examination perennially set by the USGA, and was runner-up in the US PGA three times.

And now Arnold Palmer is 50 and, sadly, not the force he once was. His swing was never one to withstand the ravages of time, as with a Littler or a Snead; it was an instrument for bludgeoning the ball, for demanding the utmost from joint and sinew and inevitably there comes a time when the demands cannot be met.

It has been said that for every dollar a player wins on the US Tour, he ought to give Palmer 25 cents. That may well be true, but we owe Arnold Palmer much more for providing us with a host of those moments similar to the one I experienced on that 1st hole at Wentworth 15 years ago. Happy Birthday, Arnold.
(1979)

HENRY COTTON

"So many people are afraid to admit they are trying – I am not." Thus, in his own words, did Henry Cotton sum up his attitude to competing at his chosen profession in an age when such an approach was considered as not quite "playing the game".

Educated at a public school – Alleyn's in Dulwich – he broke the tradition that professionals should be horny-handed sons of the soil, doffing their caps regularly at the gentry of club membership. His background equipped him with a broader view of the possibilities of success as a professional golfer and by the time he turned professional at the age of 19 in 1926, he pursued his career with a rare single-mindedness and dedication. His first job was as an assistant at Fulwell to George Oke, who was a fine club-maker, but Cotton never took to the life of serving club members and was soon after a full-time professional's post which would allow him to practise as relentlessly as possible. This he achieved when he became the professional at Langley Park, Kent in 1926 and embarked on a daily routine of hitting hundreds of balls.

Realising that the great players of the day were in America he took off to the United States at the end of 1928 to find what lay at the source of their domination. This was the era of Jones and Hagen, who monopolised the Open Championship, and during his five months there playing on the winter circuit, Cotton completely changed his swing and learned to draw the ball for greater length. This was a crucial step in his development and from then on he became the finest striker of the ball Britain had seen since the days of Vardon. The repetitiveness of his swing allied to intense concentration made him a formidable competitor, and having made his debut in the Ryder Cup in 1929 when he won the decisive single in a British victory, he then set about achieving his ambition of winning the Open Championship.

153

The Open was the one event which motivated him above all others and he geared his life from year to year to winning it. Like most players, he suffered disappointments before the goal was reached but during the Championships of the early 1930s he was creeping nearer and nearer his main objective. When the Open arrived at Royal St George's in 1934 he was in despair. He had practised until he could practise no more, had tried out four different sets of clubs and still couldn't hit the ball to his own high standards with any of them. Feeling that perhaps he was over-golfed, he didn't touch a club for the entire weekend before the Championship started and then emerged to embark on a run of the most scintillating scoring the Championship had ever seen. A pre-qualifying round of 66 at St George's was followed by one of 75 at Deal and then in the Championship itself he opened with a 67. He continued in the same vein in the second round and arrived on the 17th tee needing two fours for another 67. Instead, he finished with two threes for the score that was to become emblazoned on millions of Dunlop balls thereafter. Now nine strokes ahead of the field, he added a third round of 72 to stand on the threshold of the first British victory for 11 years. The start of his final round was delayed and in the tension of waiting he developed severe stomach cramps. He staggered to the turn in 40 strokes and appeared on the verge of collapse but a long putt for a four on the 13th stopped the rot and he eventually won by five strokes.

Hailed as the saviour of British golf, Cotton's victory inspired an unbroken run of British winners up to World War II. Not least among these was his second title in 1937 at Carnoustie, when he defeated the full might of the visiting and victorious American Ryder Cup team. The last two rounds were played in atrocious weather and at one time it was thought that play would be abandoned because of the waterlogged greens, but Cotton bestrode the course like a giant and his final round of 71 is still regarded as one of the finest ever played in the Championship. There is little doubt that but for the war he would have won more Opens yet one more victory was to come his way, at Muirfield in 1948. The highlight of this win was his second round of 66, which was a round fit for a king since it was witnessed by one, namely George VI. Now aged 41 and beginning to feel the effects of ill-health, he began to curtail his tournament appearances and in fact did not play in another Open until 1952 when he finished fourth. He won his last tournament in 1964.

Throughout his career, Cotton was always his own man. He believed that the skills he had worked so hard to hone deserved their due reward and that the public would be willing to pay for the best. He made himself a "star" in the truest sense of the word, even at one time topping the bill at the London

Coliseum with a demonstration of his swing. Inevitably, his demands that the petty rules which applied to professionals should not apply to him led him into conflicts. For example, if he were banned from the clubhouse he would, in the style of Walter Hagen, get his chauffeur to bring his lunch out to him in his car. He enjoyed the best of life and at one time had a suite at Claridges and a house in Belgravia. He was comfortable in the millionaire playgrounds of Europe and projected the image of the sleek-haired matinee idol. He knew that the press would always hang on his every word and shamelessly cultivated his relationships with them while they, equally shamelessly, allowed themselves to be cultivated. He was a lucid speaker, fluent in French, Spanish and Portuguese, a fine teacher, writer of several books and for many years a contributor to newspapers and magazines. He was an innovator, golf course architect and campaigner for the emancipation of the British golf professional. Henry Cotton never lost his enthusiasm for the game. Young professionals flocked to his villa in Portugal's Penina Hotel complex, the course he designed and where he lived for the great part of his later life. He was also responsible for starting the Golf Foundation when, in the early 1950s, he wrote to several public schools offering his services as a coach – six of those schools replied and from these modest beginnings the Golf Foundation now provides tuition for 30,000 youngsters each year.

"Putting something back into the game" is a phrase which, by today's standards, could be regarded as a cynical exercise in public relations. In Henry Cotton's case, no golfer ever put more back. His contribution was immense and it bewildered many of his friends that the accolade of a knighthood should be delayed so long. Perhaps it was because it had taken the hierarchy 50 years to realise that not being afraid to admit you are trying is as good a philosophy as can be found, not just for golf but for life itself.
(1988)

FALDO FINDS NEW RHYTHM

Nick Faldo's victory in the Spanish Open, his first since 1984, followed nearly three years of anguish as he restructured what was universally regarded as the most rhythmic swing in Europe.

That 1984 season saw Faldo make the all-important breakthrough in America when he won the Sea Pines Heritage Classic, while the year before he had dominated Europe, winning five titles and topping the money list.

Why, then, should such an obviously accomplished player subject himself to any kind of swing change? The answer lies not so much in what he had achieved but in what he might have achieved.

In the 1984 Masters, Faldo was handily placed to make a run at the title but wilted in the final round: in the Open of the same year, his first two rounds of 69 and 68 and his last of 69 were interrupted by an ugly 76, and in the US PGA he opened with a 69 and arrived at the 18th tee in the second round still contesting the lead but took an eight.

Always the perfectionist, Faldo sought to eradicate his destructive shots on the practice ground. His fellow professionals sympathised with his plight and proffered well-meaning advice. The consequence was that he became thoroughly confused, even resorting to dabbling in Scientology.

In the age of the golfing guru, Faldo had no particular mentor. He had learned to play the game under the eye of Ian Connelly back home in Welwyn Garden City, but they had long ago separated.

A chance meeting on a practice ground in America brought Faldo into contact with David Leadbetter, a Zimbabwe-born teaching professional resident in Florida. Leadbetter agreed to work with Faldo and the restructuring began.

Tall men find golf more difficult to play consistently than those of shorter stature, and at 6ft 3in Faldo was no exception. At times, his swing was too long, sometimes too short; he would use his legs too much or not enough. But the overriding problem was that he tended to tilt his shoulders rather than turn them.

Throughout the 1985 and 1986 seasons, Faldo was a somewhat unnerving sight as he stood to the ball and went through an exaggerated rolling of the forearms prior to each swing. The object of this was to remind himself to get the club up into a square position at the top. It was a painful process as in 1985 he plummeted down the European money list to 42nd, his lowest placing since his first year as a professional in 1976.

The first signs of improvement began to filter through last year; he took fifth place in the Open and, by the end of the season, had climbed back to 15th place in the European rankings.

It has been an arduous three years, during which only one man believed he was doing the right thing in changing his swing. If, among the many awards proliferating in the professional game, there was one for doggedness, Nick Faldo would surely win it.

(1987)

THE BIG THREE AND D'ARTAGNAN

Nostalgia is not what it was. But nobody over the age of 45 at St Andrews would subscribe to that idea. The fleeting images of monochrome days are here in splendid technicolor, and casting long shadows.

Arnold Palmer, Gary Player, Jack Nicklaus and Lee Trevino now represent the vanguard of golf's grey power movement, but put the scent of a major championship under their nostrils, and the years roll back. Although Player won the 1959 Open at Muirfield, it was Palmer who really took the Championship by the scruff, and dragged it into a new area.

Arriving at St Andrews 30 years ago, Palmer was on target for the Grand Slam, with the Masters and US Open already stashed away. His attempt was only foiled by some astonishing putting by Australia's Kel Nagle, but that hardened his resolve to return and seize what he considered to be rightfully his.

Beating through the gale at Royal Birkdale in 1961, Palmer secured his first title and then faced a complete contrast in conditions the following year at Troon. Dry, hard and bouncy, the Ayrshire course gave most competitors the fits, including Nicklaus, who was making his first appearance. For Palmer, however, it was a romp. Four rounds of sustained brilliance produced a new Championship aggregate record.

For Player, the winning of championships was always a tortuous business. His first victory at Muirfield set the pattern as he finished with a 68, but took six on the final hole to give himself an agonising wait. Thereafter his victories became a kind of Pilgrim's Progress, whereby he experienced his personal Slough of Despond, before emerging triumphant on the other side. He always had to feel that someone or something was out to get him.

In 1968 at Carnoustie the motivation was provided by Nicklaus. In 1974 at Royal Lytham he was driven by a different demon. Not being able to apply the chloroform rag by creeping up on his rivals from behind, as was his usual practice, Player went into the final round with a five stroke lead, and then revealed that he would much rather be a stroke behind. Having convinced himself that this in fact was his position, he took his third title.

Nothing reveals the empathy that Nicklaus has for the Open than the name he gave to his own course in his home town. Muirfield Village rolls easily off the tongue, but it could have turned out to be Lytham Village, or even, perish the thought, St Andrews Village.

At Lytham in 1963, Nicklaus finished weakly to miss the play-off between Bob Charles and Phil Rodgers by a stroke. The following year, over the Old

Course, he ran into some bad weather and a man named Tony Lema. Frustrated again at Birkdale in 1965 he began to get the feeling that destiny would not bring him together with the old claret jug.

In the hayfield that was Muirfield's rough in 1966, the moment arrived. Using his exceptional power with the longer irons, he held off the challenges of David Thomas and Doug Sanders to complete his first set of all four major championship titles.

Four years later, Nicklaus again denied Sanders after a play-off, but realistically it was Sanders who denied himself by missing that heart-breaking short putt on the final green. In 1978, Nicklaus became the third man in the history of the Open to win consecutive titles at St Andrews.

The D'Artagnan to the Three Musketeers of Palmer, Player and Nicklaus was undoubtedly Trevino. Emerging from the windblown flatlands of Texas, he had evolved a swing that was entirely suited to the perfidiousness of links golf. Trevino chuckled his way round Birkdale in 1971 to win his first Open. His victory the next year at Muirfield was less amusing for British golf followers, as he destroyed the ambitions of Tony Jacklin in outrageous fashion. God was a Mexican in 1972, and life for the illegitimate son of a gravedigger had never been sweeter.

All good things must come to an end, however. Palmer has declared that this has been his last appearance in the Open, thereby gracefully conceding to the march of time. Player has set himself the target of becoming the first man to win a major championship in his fifties, but while his spirit is beyond question, the physical demands are now too great.

Nicklaus is still strong enough to cope with today's lengthening courses, but has yet to come to terms with the latest milestone in his age. Coming from the school of hard knocks, Trevino is content to take whatever bonuses the game and the Senior Tour can generate.

Each of them has, in his own way, added lustre to a golden age. The boyhood heroes of yesteryear may be bouncing their grandchildren on their knee, but for those who saw them in their pomp, the memories never fade. (1990)

WHY DO WE DRAG DOWN THE WORLD'S TOP PLONKER?

"They wound up the mechanical man of golf and sent him clicking round the course." Those words were applied to Bobby Jones when the great American amateur was virtually unbeatable during the 1920s.

Now it is time to take them down and dust them off again because the clockwork repetitiveness of Nick Faldo's swing justifies no better description.

The mechanic to Faldo's Formula One methods is David Leadbetter, the lanky Zimbabwean instructor who surveys his pupil from under a large peaked cap, making sure the engine never misses a stroke. Theirs is a relationship forged through hours on the practice ground over the past five years and, while it may appear that Faldo's performance at St Andrews was the pinnacle, both men believe that greater heights can be scaled.

This attitude leaves British sport lovers feeling faintly uneasy. Weaned on a diet of narrow but glorious failure, we are used to overseas competitors adopting a dedicated win-at-all-costs approach, but find it hard to accept in our own product.

What other country, for example, would provide a comfortable retirement for two horizontal heavyweight boxers and pay good money for one of them to advertise a particularly pungent aftershave lotion, and the other to appear in a Christmas pantomime?

If we do produce a sporting genius, then he or she should be flawed. Nothing appears to satisfy the British public more than building someone up and then knocking them down. The shooting star syndrome has embraced such performers as George Best, Ian Botham, Alex Higgins and Tony Jacklin among others, all of whom at one time or another pressed the self-destruct button but were all hounded by the tabloid pack until sometimes they could take no more.

And the pack keeps finding fresh quarry. Unable to find an acceptable quote from Faldo himself, who is naturally wary of newspapermen, they latched on to Scott Hoch. Hoch, whose relationship with Faldo has not exactly been all beer and skittles since the 1989 US Masters, was unwise enough to provide a taped interview in which he claimed that Faldo was aloof, unfriendly and disliked by his fellow professionals on both sides of the Atlantic.

"We hate Faldo" and "Nasty Nick" were just two examples of the response to Hoch's comments, while one unwittingly came out with something approaching accuracy when its headline ran: "Faldo is a plonker."

He is, indeed. He plonks it down the fairway, he plonks it on the green and he plonks it in the hole.

All this arrived with Faldo's breakfast marmalade on the day he was due to set off in pursuit of the greatest prize in world golf. Whether he reads this rubbish or not, the fact it is there is a sad reflection on the society which does appear to want to read it.

Faldo is no swashbuckler in the Palmer-Ballesteros mould. His golf does not provide that rollercoaster of emotion which goes with daring recoveries and death-defying carries. It is too consistent for that. He is more comparable with Ben Hogan in his clinical approach and his ruthless destruction of par.

The trouble is that we always want more. We want our man to be a winner but we also want him to be able to crack a joke and raise a laugh. As a stand-up comic, Faldo couldn't even come close to being Lee Trevino's straight man, nor would he want to be.

Instead, he is by universal acclaim the best player in the world – unless you believe the rankings of a Japanese electrical manufacturer – but he is certainly Britain's most successful sportsman.

It is worth remembering that both Hogan and Jack Nicklaus only became revered figures in the game through their monumental achievements within it. They, too, lacked instant appeal, but people still ask: "Did you ever see Hogan play?"

One day, they will say the same of Nicklaus, and it is Nick Faldo's most fervent wish that, later on, people will say the same of him. We should all be grateful for that.

(1990)

GORILLA IN THE MIDST

Perhaps the oldest joke in golf concerns the man who arrives to play a round accompanied by a gorilla.

On the 1st tee, in front of a curious crowd of onlookers, the gorilla drives to the green 500 yards away, whereupon one of the stunned spectators asks: "How does he putt?" "About the same," replies the gorilla's owner, "500 yards."

Now the joke is almost reality, for at Crooked Stick in the US PGA Championship the gorilla, disguised as John Daly, struck back. With a driver made from the latest space-age material, Daly produced tee shots which would not have been out of place at Cape Kennedy.

But making a monkey out of the world's elite requires more than just progidious hitting and in this respect Daly was equally arresting.

Not for him the prowling and scowling that is the norm from professionals facing a tricky chip or putt; instead he was refreshingly quick, taking one look before giving the ball a healthy rap.

A total of 21 birdies and one eagle in 72 holes bears testimony to this approach and if a player is building this much credit to his account, then the odd double bogey debit is not going to hurt too badly.

The question now arises as to whether Daly is simply a one tournament wonder or the most thrilling natural talent to emerge since Severiano Ballesteros? That he has a talent for powerful striking there's no doubt, and, given the right sort of course and conditions, he will win again. What he might do to Augusta next April hardly bears thinking about.

The evidence from Crooked Stick, however, suggests that Daly has not yet acquired the full repertoire of strokes needed to tackle any course in any kind of conditions.

Such a strong right to left game may cause its owner problems in high winds on a tight course. It remains to be seen whether he can hit a low punch shot left to right in a right to left wind and hold the ball straight. Will he be able to fade and hook the ball to order, particularly when the pressure is at its most intense?

It has always been the case that powerful players can be straightened out, while it is difficult to imbue power if it is not already there. Daly's back-swing with every club, not just the driver, resembles a man in a shower trying to scratch an inaccessible part of his body with a loofah. And the first thing any teacher would do is try to shorten it.

This may be the last thing Daly wants, for at the moment he is a good old boy having fun with a golf ball. On a circuit where swings are cloned and visors are the standard headgear, the Daly swing and the Daly haircut stand out.

I hope he does something about the haircut and the straggly blond moustache, but, really, I hope he leaves the swing alone. There are enough players out there grooving the perfect swing, reducing it to the minimum of moving parts and approaching the game as if it were some advanced form of trigonometry.

Certainly Daly may take 90 on occasions, but there will be other times when he spread-eagles the opposition the same as he did at Crooked Stick.

Nobody would say that Arnold Palmer was a model of orthodoxy when he first burst on the scene and he, too, was capable of touching the extremes in terms of scoring.

Given that Daly may just be the new standard-bearer of American golf, it is surprising that he has not been picked for the Ryder Cup. To play a match against someone who hits the ball that far must be soul-destroying, even if you are a hardened professional, and in four-ball play he would be devastating.

By selecting Ray Floyd and Chip Beck, US captain Dave Stockton has gone for experience rather than flair and, I believe, relinquished an initiative which Daly created.

The propensity that club golfers have for trying to emulate the top professionals' swings will surely have to be resisted in the case of John Daly. A friend of mine tried it the other day. There was an ominous click and he should be able to hit a few chips and putts in about a month's time. (1991)

SWINGING THE IRISH WAY

Irish golf suffered a double blow recently with the death of two of its favourite sons, Harry Bradshaw and Fred Daly.

Although Bradshaw was from the south and Daly the north, such division counts for nothing in golf and the two of them provided enormous pleasure for people of all denominations.

It is almost a tradition that Irish golfers do not conform to any of the technical orthodoxies laid down in the instruction manuals and Bradshaw and Daly were no exception.

Bradshaw ambled on to the tee looking like a character from a pork pie commercial. Stout and ruddy-faced, he always wore a cap pulled down so far over his face that he had to tilt his head back to see where he was going. His grip would have had the Leadbetters of this world seeking alternative employment as he overlapped the last three fingers of his right hand, leaving just the forefinger on the club.

The swing, if it can be called such, obviously had its origins in shinty but those massive hands invariably sent the ball unerringly down the middle and around the greens he was an absolute wizard.

Although he won a number of tournaments, Bradshaw will be remembered chiefly as the victim of one of the most curious incidents in the history of the Open Championship.

At Royal St George's in 1949, at the 5th hole on the second round, his ball came to rest against, not inside as is usually recalled, a broken bottle. In these days of automatic free drops it seems ludicrous that he did not seek a ruling but, unsure of his rights, he decided to play the ball as it lay. He smashed ball and bottle, the former some 15 yards up the fairway, completed the hole in six and the round in 77.

He tied for first place with Bobby Locke but was slaughtered in the play-off. It could be said that Bradshaw was the only man who failed to win the Open by not losing his bottle.

Daly did win the Open and remains the only Irishman to have done so. At Hoylake in 1947 he set a target of 293 which the later starters could not match although Frank Stranahan, the great American amateur, nearly holed his second shot at the final hole to tie.

Daly was not a big man and consequently had to strive for length. To assist in this quest he used clubs which were two inches longer than standard and a driver that weighed 17 ounces. Perhaps because of the weight and length of his clubs, his backswing contained a pronounced sway with the club well past the horizontal, but he was a wonderfully straight hitter.

His putting method contained a fair amount of 'Irishness' in that he glanced sideways at the hole several times before hitting the ball and at the same time whistled between his teeth.

However eccentric Bradshaw and Daly's swings were, they were models of orthodoxy compared with that of James Bruen. By all accounts Bruen hit the ball phenomenally long distances and his power was achieved in a way you might like to try the next time you play.

You turn your body in the normal way but as you raise the club you keep it pointing at the tee marker. At the completion of the turn you still keep the club pointing horizontally at the tee marker, then you loop back inside and down into the ball.

This really is like a man killing snakes and while most of us using this method would end up in the infirmary, for Bruen it created a tremendous whiplash effect that occasionally resulted in him snapping the shaft on the downswing. He won the Amateur Championship in 1946 but the strain this method placed on his wrists eventually forced him into early retirement.

The Irish tradition has been well maintained by the likes of Christy O'Connor senior, who almost let go of the club at the top of the swing before grabbing it again in time to hit the ball; Joe Carr, who stood to the ball like a giraffe going down to drink; and Jimmy Kinsella, a player who used a driver with two shafts, one hammered inside the other, and who had a backswing which made Doug Sanders look like Ben Crenshaw.

Of the modern era of Irish players, Eamonn Darcy continues down the non-conformist route with a swing that is almost Bruenesque in its execution; Ronan Rafferty has a little drum majorette twirl at the top; and Des Smyth swings like an out-of-control windmill.

The best of the current crop, however, is a grave disappointment in that he possesses a swing so perfectly in plane that it is a joy to behold. His name is David Feherty and he is going to be worth watching in 1991.
(1991)

Unmatched Set

Test Your Dedication as a Golfer

Golf is one of those games which you embrace wholeheartedly or discard altogether – there is no room for half-measures.

That is how it should be, but some people put other things such as work, career, the family, or even the ability to be fluent in seven different languages before the pursuit of excellence on the golf course. This exceedingly dangerous faction must be rooted out before it taints those who are dedicated golfers.

This simple test will tell you whether you are suited to continue to play golf or whether your time would be better spent translating the Maastricht Treaty into Serbo-Croat.

1. It is Christmas Eve and you have managed to get out of the office party. You have arranged a four-ball with your usual cronies but as you leave for the club you remember that you haven't bought your wife a present.

   Do you:
   (a) Rush back into the house, phone your friends and cancel your game?
   (b) Stop off on your way to the club and buy her a box of chocolates?
   (c) Play your game and then buy her a dozen golf balls from the professional's shop knowing that she has never played golf in her life?

2. You've just broken 80 for the first time in your life. As you walk into the bar, someone asks you how you got on.

   Do you:
   (a) Mutter something modest like "Not too badly"?
   (b) Smile enigmatically?
   (c) Lead the questioner to a corner, take out your card and go through it with him, drive by drive, iron shot by iron shot and putt by putt?

3. You are on a fact-finding trade mission to Japan. As part of your tour you are taken to see examples of the Japanese art of Bonsai. You are admiring a particular tree which your guide tells you is a persimmon.

Do you:

(a) Ask how long it takes for the tree to mature?

(b) Marvel at the hours of work it takes to produce such a beautiful specimen?

(c) Say "That's what they make wooden clubs from"?

4. Your wife is a regular church-goer but she is distressed that, because of your golf, you rarely attend any services. She asks the vicar to have a chat with you about it.

When the vicar calls do you:

(a) Repent immediately and promise to change your ways?

(b) Pour him a large Scotch and tell him about your wife's apparent attack of religious mania?

(c) Tell him that, come to think of it, you haven't seen much of him at the golf club lately?

5. You are visited by the Devil, who proposes that in exchange for your soul you can have one round of golf over the Old Course at St Andrews in which you will set a course record of 61 in a match against Severiano Ballesteros.

Do you:

(a) Refuse point blank?

(b) Tell him that he ought to be aware that Ballesteros is cutting back his schedule?

(c) Accept on condition that the match is televised and you are allowed to go around in 59?

6. Your knowledge of the mechanics of golf swing could be could be written on a pinhead but, on passing the practice ground, you see a player slicing every shot into the next parish.

Do you:

(a) Pass by on the other side?

(b) Go over and tell him he ought to see the professional?

(c) Go over and start advising your own theories, ending up by hitting the remainder of his practice balls yourself?

7. You are practising your putting in the office when the company chairman walks in and asks what on earth you think you are doing.

Do you:

(a) Apologise profusely?

(b) Mutter something about an important client's meeting with old so-and-so, who's mad on golf?

(c) Tell him that his damned carpet putts too fast and it's time he bought one with a deeper pile?

8. It is a lovely summer's evening and you are out having a quiet practice round by yourself. On one hole you slice your drive into some tall grass and on arriving in the vicinity of your shot you see your ball lying a few feet away from a couple entwined in what can only be termed a compromising position. As you get nearer, you realise that the couple are your wife and the club secretary.

Do you:

(a) Retreat quickly hoping you haven't been seen?

(b) Demand to know the meaning of this liaison?

(c) Go up to your ball, take out a club and ask the secretary whether he regards himself and his companion as loose impediments or immovable obstructions?

9. You are playing alone and have a hole-in-one. The only witness to your piece of good fortune is a man out walking his dog who then starts to walk away.

Do you:

(a) Resign yourself to the fact that your feat will go unrecognised?

(b) Take the man's name and address and say you'll get in touch later?

(c) Club him unconscious with your driver and drag him back to the secretary's office?

(1992)

A Pro–Amme Tale
(With Apologies To Chaucer)

This winter and its icie blasts
Our thoughts to sunnie spottes doth caste.
But where to go, thatte is the nub,
To playye our gayme and to rubbe
The sun-tanne lotion on our bakkes.
And free of cares of income taxxe,
We sporte among the palm-frynged glaydes
To gette a tanne which never faydes.
The choice is wyde and to be faire,
Halfe of the funne is gettying there.
And so to Heathrowe did I wende
With clubbes, balles, monie to spende,
To fynde my baggage, when t'was weighed,
Was in excess – I payd and payd
A fortune 'fore I caught the flygthe
Thatte was to wing me thru the nyghte.
For thirteen houres I was goyng
Across the sea, inside a Boeyng,
With in-flyghte move (which I'd seene),
Before we landed inne the Caribbean.
There was a courier among our lotte
And he announced thatte we had gotte
To fille an immigration forme
With name and number, t'was the norme.
And then he tolde us of the place
Thatte we were goyng to apace.
Of drinkes thatte were onne the house.
Of locale dishes – 'Curried Mouse'
Was one favoured by a fewe,
Though eares and whiskers were hard to chewe.
Then from our groupe there came a crie:
"Please let me thru, I'm going to die."
And downe the gangways there he ranne
Towards the tail-end and Elsanne.
The courier he shooke his head.

"It gettes to some of them" he said,
And then a brochure he did showe
Of sunnie beaches, far from snowe.
We looked atte it, then looked again.
T'was not the Caribbean, it was Spain!
Up spake a lawyer from our groupe:
"Looke here, my manne, how dare you stoope
To such a trick – kindly explaine.
Why not the Caribbean instead of Spain?"
The courier, he took the floore.
"It's what we call a mystery tour."
And then, inne a much louder voyce:
"You payes your monie and you takes your choyce.
It could be Portugal but inne the mayne
We usually ende uppe in Spain."
T'was a professional who spake up next:
"Excuse me sir, but I am vexed
The Caribbean holds my thrall
Not Spain nor bluddy Portugal."
The uproar grewe as people swore
And stamped their feete upon the floore
With cryes of "Court Line" and "On yer bike"
And other wordes you would not like.
And while the shoutyng was atte its peake
The pilot's voyce beganne to speake
Via the internal radyo relay.
"Ladyes and Gentlemenne, I'm sorry to saye
We've developed a fault, the plane will remaine
And not go to the Caribbean, Portugal nor Spain.
Please disembark quietly, the stewardess will lead onne
To airport hotels, Ariel and Sheratonne."
And so we left, somewhatte down-hearted
The trippe was over before we'd departed.
But then, as I've quothed, when all's said and done
When it comes to travail, gettyng there is halfe the funne.
(1980)

CAUGHT ON THE REBOUND

Considering the number of golf balls struck during a year it would be a mammoth task to work out the odds of being struck by someone else's misguided missile. However lengthy those odds might be, they would shorten considerably if one took into account the number of times a player was struck by his own ball.

Rebounds and ricochets are all part of golf's guerrilla warfare: those occasions when we venture deep into the jungle and, on locating our ball, are determined to explore the scientific conundrum that trees are 90 per cent air. Ninety per cent of the time we discover that trees are 100 per cent wood and we have to take evasive action.

Sometimes that action is not evasive enough, as was recently demonstrated by Brett Ogle in the Australian Open. On the 17th hole on the final round, Ogle decided to test the tree/air equation and was felled when his ball rebounded and struck him on the knee. "XXXX!" said Ogle, as his knee was packed in cans of the sponsor's ice-cold product.

In addition to the hair-line fracture his knee suffered, Ogle's score was also severely damaged as he eventually holed out in nine, including a two-stroke penalty for being struck by his own ball.

The other area where rebounds are prevalent is bunkers. Is there a golfer who has not found the ball under the lip of a bunker, hit it and heard that sickening thud as it strikes the bank in front? This is then followed by a split second of complete unawareness as to the ball's whereabouts before realisation dawns as it curves gently downwards before plummeting onto your foot.

This happened in the 1979 English Amateur Championship at Royal St George's. Reg Glading, that stalwart of Surrey golf for so many years, was involved in a match which went into extra holes. On the 22nd, or fourth extra hole, his drive pitched into the cavernous bunker which guards the right-hand side of the fairway.

He found his ball had plugged right at the top of this immense dune. Glading clambered up to his ball with a club, made fast his stance, took a swing and over-balanced, falling back some 25 feet to the bottom. The ball followed him down, struck him and he had to concede the hole and the match.

In terms of spectacular and expensive rebounds, few can match one which occurred in the African country of Benin. Factory worker Mathieu Boya was practising during his lunch break in a field next to the country's main air base. A slightly off-centre stroke sent a ball over the dividing fence where it hit a bird. The bird crashed down and went straight through the windscreen of a jet that was about to take off.

The pilot was unable to prevent his aircraft crashing into four other jets parked on the runway, thereby destroying the country's air force. Police arrested Mr Boya, presented him with a bill for £26 million and asked him what he was going to do about it. Mr Boya replied that he was going to strengthen his left-hand grip.

In 40 years of playing golf I have twice been hit by a ball other than my own. The first occasion was in the 1950s when I was a schoolboy and was playing in a foursome at Frilford Heath. Standing at the side of one tee watching my partner drive, I was struck on the ankle by one that came straight off the toe of the club.

Since my partner was the son of the man who made the famous "Cotton Oxford" shoes I was able to dine out on the fact that I had been struck by a ball hit by Cotton.

The second time occurred on the 17th of the High Course at Moor Park when I was knocked out by a ball struck from the 16th tee. I came to and found the frantic figure of Bruce Forsyth dancing in attendance, for it was he who had hit me. "Are you all right, my love?" he asked. With that I gave a groan and promptly blacked out again.

(1991)

THE UNIVERSAL RULE

Citizens of the United Kingdom not resident abroad are subject to a variety of laws and regulations, the purpose of which it would appear is to keep the legal profession in happy and contented luxury.

But in addition to the laws which govern the air we breathe, the speed at which we travel and the size of our income tax bill, there are other unwritten laws which, as we travel down life's potholed road, become increasingly evident.

The laws could be defined collectively under the heading of Universal Rules, sub-headed Sod's Law, the principle of which is that if it can possibly go wrong it will, and even if it can't it might.

Sod's Law decrees that when we are stuck in a five-mile tailback on the M1, the radio will warn us to avoid the M1 because there is a five-mile tailback. It also decrees that while we are in that traffic jam, the lane we are in will remain immobile while vehicles in the other lanes stream past us, and if we switch lanes, then that lane suddenly comes to a juddering halt.

But there is no field of human endeavour more ideally suited to the application of Sod's Law than golf. A game based on self-delusion with disappointment lurking round the corner of every dog-leg has to be the ultimate in proving that if it can possibly go wrong it will and even if it can't it might.

Consider for a moment what happens when we play golf and when professionals play. We, in our ineptitude, are capable of hitting the ball to all four points of the compass while the professionals are more used to hitting the ball in the direction they require.

Yet it is they who have the protective wall of humanity lining each fairway and surrounding every green to prevent their ball from running into trouble. Furthermore, should the crowd part like the Red Sea to allow a professional's ball to run deep into the woods, the professional not only has room for a full swing but also has a gap towards the green. You or I would, if we found our ball, need an earthquake to give us room to swing and create the gap.

Consider also the fate of the career shot. There we are in the middle of the fairway, on a hanging lie, facing a long iron shot through a strong left-to-right wind to a plateau green with the pin tucked in on the left-hand side.

Scorning the prudence of all coaching manuals to play within our limits, we select a 2-iron and strike the ball witheringly through the tempest with just a hint of draw. The ball lands on the green, exactly on line with the flag.

Our friends gather round to heap congratulations upon us. As we approach the green, the ball recedes further and further away from the pin until, when we finally reach it, we discover the green has three tiers, the ball is on the lower one, the pin is on the top. This is known as Sod's Law of Golfing Optics, defined as nothing ever finishes as close as originally thought and even if it does it is never as close as we would like.

Finally, there is the Lone Bush Attraction or Sod's Law of Unerring Accuracy.

This was brought home to me with a vengeance while playing over the West Course at Wentworth. Following a reasonable drive down the 18th fairway, I prudently elected to place my second shot in the left half of the fairway, thereby leaving me a simple pitch on to the green. Note the use of the word "simple" for it is integral to the self-deception, bearing in mind that the only simple thing about golf is that it is relatively easy to spell.

Before I struck the shot, I noticed a small tree or bush on the edge of the left-hand rough, a solitary growth which appeared out of place among the glorious chestnuts and oaks beyond it.

I struck the ball, it wavered not an inch from its intended path. I watched it land and roll forward and I knew exactly where it had finished. The tree itself was an old Christmas offering, long since removed from the clubhouse, barely alive but sufficiently tall and bushy to shroud my ball from further forward progress. At times like these one is tempted to fall on one's knees and cry: "Why me, oh Lord, why me?" But what's the use? In golf, as in life, the Universal Rule always gets you in the end.
(1984)

AN EVERYDAY STORY OF COUNTRY CLUB FOLK

Background music of birds singing, interspersed with noise of club striking ball, followed by muffled oaths.

Walter Gabriel Basher (a rustic): 'Ello Dan, me old pal, me old beauty, 'ow you be goin' on then?

Dan Basher (a local farmer): Fair to middlin' Walter, fair to middlin'. The course be right crowded at the moment but you should get a game around milkin' time.

Walter Gabriel Basher: I tell 'ee Dan, you were right sensible to listen to some of me homespun philosophisin' about the rotation of crops. Didn't I tell 'ee to stop plantin' barley, wheat and rye and concentrate on Captain's Day, Societies and the monthly medal?

Dan Basher: That you did Walter, that you did.

Walter Gabriel Basher: Aaar, and it's beginnin' to pay off to my way of thinkin' (*Pause while Walter lights pipe*). That looks like young Phil comin' through 40-acre hollow.

Dan Basher: That's him, Walter. He went off first – he'll be finished in a moment.

Walter Gabriel Basher: Him look to be gurt muttocked if you arsk me. Who 'ee be a-playin' with then?

Dan Basher: That's young Gwen Pitcher, daughter of the Squire.

Walter Gabriel Basher: She'm got lovely big headcovers. I'll warrant there's not a finer pair in the whole of Ambridge.

Sound of footsteps approaching:

Phil Basher: Hello Dad, hello Walter.

Dan Basher: Hello son, how did you get on?

Phil Basher: Not too bad – level par but I dropped a couple round 40-acre hollow.

Walter Gabriel Basher: Aaar, that always was a right vexing piece of land. What I allus say is if you match par round 40-acre hollow a thicky score is bound to follow.

Phil Basher: Away with you, Walter, and your homespun philosophising. Well, I must be off, I've got a meeting with the man from the EEC Commission on golf courses.

Footsteps fade, cue in sound of clattering crockery.

Doris Basher: It's nice of you to help me, Gwen. We've got to lay for 80 lunches and I'm fair twittered I can tell you. How are you and young Phil getting along?

Gwen Pitcher: Oh, Mrs Basher, he's so wrapped up in his golf I'm not sure if it's me he loves or my big headcovers. The other day I hit my ball into Badger's Glade and we were getting quite cosy looking for it when he suddenly jumped up and said I'd had my five minutes and I should go back and play another.

Doris Basher: The Basher men are all the same, love. I had the same trouble with my Dan when we were courting. You've got to remember the way to a man's heart is through his long iron. Now, we'd better get on with these lunches.

Cue in to Dan and Walter back at the golf course.

Walter Gabriel Basher: 'Ello Dan, me old pal, me old beauty, you be lookin' like a man who's just shanked out of bounds.

Dan Basher: Young Phil has just finished his meeting with the man from the EEC Commission on golf courses. We've got to increase our quota. Last month we only had 2,500 rounds played which, according to the EEC directive, is 20 per cent below the set figure as laid out in sub-section 29, paragraph 16, clause 11. I just don't know how we're going to do it – the course is crowded enough as it is.

Walter Gabriel Basher: Don't 'ee worry Dan, me old pal, me old beauty. Walter will come up with summat.

Dan Basher: Looks like it might rain.

Walter Gabriel Basher: Aaar, it do that. What I allus say is if golfers do stand out in the rain, look out for wet golfers.

Dan Basher: Walter.

Walter Gabriel Basher: Yes Dan.

Dan Basher: I've got a piece of homespun philosophising for you.

Walter Gabriel Basher: What's that Dan, me old pal, me old beauty?

Dan Basher: Why don't you sod off?

Cue in music.
Voice Over: You have been listening to the Bashers, an everyday story of country club folk.
(1990)

GOLFER'S GUIDE TO THE GREENHOUSE EFFECT

Golf and gardening are, in my book anyway, incompatible. One involves physical co-ordination: the other physical exhaustion.

But even non-gardening golfers will know that the growing season is upon us, if only for the fact that golf balls display a greater propensity for vanishing in the thickening rough.

Golfers of a horticultural bent, however, know that nature's bounty can be found everywhere and that golf courses are inhabited by many rare and exotic species worth closer examination.

This brief guide tells you what to look for as well as providing information on pruning, fertilising and weed and pest control.

Nicklaus Jackmanii (*Ursus d'Oro*): Popularly known as the Ursus D'Oro, the Nicklaus Jackmanii was for many years the dominant plant in the plot, superceding the perennial favourite Latrobe Delight (*Palmeris chargum*).

Other plants, such as Miller's Flash (*Mormonia*) and Kansas Star (*Watsonia*) tried to outgrow the Ursus D'Oro and enjoyed brief spells of popularity. But the influence of this plant and the spread of its branches discouraged extended growth from other flowering shrubs.

Spanish Superstar (*Ballesteros grandiflorum*): A flamboyant, Iberian climber, Spanish Superstar takes well in most soils but thrives mainly in Europe, where it has won many show prizes.

Has been successfully transplanted in America, where it has caused some resentment among local growers. Regarded by many as the most exciting plant in the world, Spanish Superstar needs another major horticultural prize to confirm its status.

Thomson Supreme (*Antipodean culturus*): Noted for its simplicity and ability to cope with all conditions, Thomson Supreme first gained recognition in Britain in the early 1950s and in the space of 12 years won the Royal & Ancient Horticultural Society Gold Medal on five occasions.

It was felt that Thomson Supreme would never take to American soil conditions, but it was successfully transplanted in the States, where it enjoyed a spell of success among the older plants.

Allissum (*Commentatus urbanum*): Once a main feature plant on British courses, the Allissum died out in the early 1970s, only to reappear in a different guise.

Now flourishes in high places, where the rarified air has given it a new lease of life as it sets a fine example to other high-altitude plants by its measured growth. Blossoms freely from April to October, when its mellifluous scent fills thousands of homes.

Wild Crenshaw (*Driver erraticus*): Great things were expected from the Wild Crenshaw when it first appeared in America in the mid-1970s. But its penchant for taking root in undiscovered parts of the course severely restricted its development. Some experts recommended a cutting back of its overlong stems, but this proved unsuccessful and the plant is best left alone.

Dimpled Spheroid (*Surlynus compressum*): The Dimpled Spheroid is easily the most popular plant of any course in the world, where it is found in profusion.

Recommended habitat is closely-mown grass but the Dimpled Spheroid has a will of its own and is frequently found in the most inhospitable spots. Available in packs of three, the Dimpled Spheroid stores well in the winter but tends to run riot in the summer.

Cleveland Weevil (*Agenta internationalus*): The Cleveland Weevil feeds on richly-flowering plants, where its presence is reputed to reduce growth by 25 per cent.

It is now so well established throughout the world that there is little hope of eliminating it, though certain plants, such as Spanish Superstar, have proved resistant. Regular spraying with a specially formulated chemical called "independence" can be effective.

Flowering Shank or Lucy Locket: Dreaded growth which appears without warning with low-growing shoots which veer suddenly to the right.

Can be eliminated by extensive course of Leadbetter, the analytical controller that is also recommended for Hook (*Sinister vulgaris*), the low-growing, free-running, left-shooting weed, and Slice (*Dexter frondissii*), the tall-growing, weak-stemmed weed found on courses everywhere.
(1991)

UNLUCKY FOR SOME

Those of you fortunate enough to be reading this will know that luck on the golf course is always proportionate to the way you are playing. When you are playing well, your ball is guided, as if by some mystic hand, past all the trouble, hopping merrily over cavernous bunkers, skipping gaily out of the woods and behaving in an acceptable manner.

On the darker side of the coin, when you are playing badly that same unseen force seems to take a perverse delight in plugging your ball under the face of every bunker, plunging it into the deepest, most impenetrable rough while setting you up for commitment to the nearest asylum.

There are more hard luck stories in golf than in probably any other pastime. What is also true is that for every tale of misfortune there is an opposite story of good fortune, as encapsulated by the old saying: "Every bad shot brings pleasure to somebody."

It has also been said that good players make their own luck, but you may be surprised at the length to which some of the most famous names in the game will go to ensure that the luck stays with them.

Superstition is as rife among the stars as it is among the ordinary club golfers.

Take Jack Nicklaus, for example: when he's putting on his shoes and socks before a round they have to go on in a set sequence or else it's hardly worth him going out to play. Other Nicklaus quirks include a lucky penny for marking his ball on the green and an aversion to anything flying overhead while he is about to play a shot.

In the 1978 Open Championship at St Andrews, Nicklaus stood over his second shot to the 16th in the final round and then suddenly stepped away. Two crows were squabbling overhead and the great man revealed afterwards the he perceived the birds as an omen of bad luck and had to wait until they had flown away. He birdied the hole to set up his third Open title.

Some golfers will never play with a certain numbered ball. Bobby Locke would never play a ball with the number three on it because he felt it would make him three-putt. Severiano Ballesteros always plays a No. 1 ball.

Nick Faldo, and before him Brian Huggett, never cut their fingernails during a tournament, though this is based more on the belief that nail-cutting takes away the feel from the fingers.

Other players believe astrological forces have a bearing on their performance and consult the stars. In the 1973 US Open, American professional John

Schlee found his moon was in the ascendancy. It took an inspired final round of 63 from Johnny Miller to prevent Schlee being the star.

Of course, the one stroke in golf where luck plays a major part is a hole-in-one. Even if you carry a bag full of four-leaf clovers, horseshoes and charms, these are no guarantee of that single stroke of perfection.

While a hole-in-one is a joyous moment, fate can still lurk with the sand-filled sock ready to deliver to the base of the skull. Consider the case of the golfer who holed in one and then, while walking to the next tee, was knocked unconscious by a ball driven by another player on the hole he had just aced.

Take heed too of the circumstances surrounding a certain Dr Tucker who, in 1936, put his name down for a hole-in-one competition. He then went to the competition hole, put a ball down and holed in one. He rushed back to the clubhouse to claim his prize only to find that the competition was not due to begin for another two weeks.

When it comes to superstition, you either believe in it or your don't. The only time a black cat crossed my path I had to swerve to avoid it and nearly wrote the car off against a tree: while I was buying a lucky sprig of heather from a gypsy, her comrade in crime was gently lifting my wallet and when I opened the window to avoid looking at a new moon through glass, I was soaked by a sudden squall.

As for Friday the 13th, it's just another day, unless you are the unlikelily named Helen Bopp, from Arizona. On Friday February 13, 1981, she was playing on the Villa De Paz course and broke her arm while taking a practice swing. Where did this accident occur? On the 13th hole of course. You have been warned.

(1992)

RABID SUPPORT

One of the chief requirements for a career in journalism is that its exponents should be able to stand back from a situation, assess it carefully and report it objectively (pause for hollow laughter).

There must be neither bias nor preferential treatment. Impartiality must rule so that the reader, having been presented with the facts, can make a measured, reasoned judgement on the issue in question.

All of which is baloney whichever way you slice it. Impartiality has never been one of my strongest points, especially when sport is involved.

Take soccer for example. A pox I cry, on Manchester United, may Liverpool fall over their own bootlaces and, as for Arsenal, I can hardly write their name without thinking of something loathsome creeping out from under a stone.

Yes, you've guessed it, I'm a dyed-in-the-wool Tottenham supporter and have been since the days of Arthur Rowe and push and run. I have still yet to see a more cultured player than Danny Blanchflower or a more accomplished goalscorer than Jimmy Greaves and, while there have been lean spells in our association, the Spurs and I are destined to go marching on until I cry "Hallelujah" at the turnstiles of Heaven. I hope I don't go to the other place; it's bound to be full of Arsenal supporters.

Cricket rouses the passions rather less, for Lord's is hardly the place for vociferous support. But again the impartiality flies out of the window whenever Middlesex are playing – a legacy from the days when D C S Compton went down on one knee and swept every other batsman to mediocrity.

Any clash between the two universities will find me fiercely critical of any efforts by the team wearing that pale, rather effete, blue colour.

Being a southerner I have, of course, developed a disdainful curled lip for any sporting achievements that may occur north of Watford and I firmly believe that Geoffrey Boycott and Yorkshire County Cricket Club deserve each other, though whether we deserve Boycott's Test match commentary is another matter.

Knowing that God is an Englishman leaves me indifferent to the efforts of those people of Celtic origin and, even though the Scots, the Welsh and the Irish may on occasions defeat us, my faith in our inherent superiority remains unmoved.

The trouble is I just can't help taking sides. If I am driving through the countryside and come across a cricket or soccer match being played in some remote village I have to stop and watch.

After a few minutes I have decided which of the teams shall receive my favours and then I become its most partisan supporter.

You would think that all this favouritism would disappear when faced with an individual sport like golf, but no. While the game tends to break down national barriers, I still find myself rooting unashamedly for certain players to win, and I suffer dreadful agonies if they don't.

I still remember the pain of Arnold Palmer's defeat by Jack Nicklaus in the play-off for the 1962 US Open at Oakmont. It was almost unthinkable that Palmer, the man who turned the game into a version of unarmed combat, could lose to an overweight, crew-cut college boy.

Even in that defeat I consoled myself with the fact that, over the 72 holes, Palmer three-putted seven times while Nicklaus three-putted only once – therefore Palmer was clearly the better player.

Supporting Palmer in those days enabled me to run the full gamut of the emotions, which I suppose is what support is all about.

I still feel that he won four US Open titles, for aside from his victory in 1960, he tied for the Championship on three occasions and the play-offs, all of which he lost, were merely 18-hole lotteries in which anything could happen.

In recent years, though, I have found that my emotions regarding golfers are not tugged so readily. Perhaps this is an indication that cynicism has finally taken root, or maybe there just isn't anybody around to stoke the fires of passionate support.

I would still go a long way to see Severiano Ballesteros play, but even he stirs my feelings only occasionally.

It took me some time to come to terms with the fact that the Ryder Cup would be contested between the Americans and a European team, but eventually the old cloven hoof of chauvinism trod firmly on my attitude.

What did it matter that I was watching the son of a Bavarian bricklayer and a former Iberian caddie taking on the Americans – the important thing was they were playing for us and winning.

If sport cannot arouse the emotions of those who watch it, if the preference for a certain performer does not exist, then what is being played is merely a charade.

Occasionally sport is presented in this fashion, particularly in its canned, television guise. But in its real form, when the competition means something, it provides the senses with a keener edge rarely found elsewhere.

If you can enjoy that feeling, then why on earth shouldn't I?

(1990)

2001: A GOLF PROPHECY

As the dust settles on yet another Open Championship, it seems an appropriate time to reflect on some of the changes that have occurred in an event which has been in existence for 141 years.

With the passing of the years one's memory tends to fade but I can still remember the first Open I attended (can it really be 44 years ago?) in 1957 when Bobby Locke won at what was then known as St Andrews. Even in those far off days Locke was regarded as something of an anachronism, for he persisted in wearing what were known as plus-fours, which were trousers that finished just below the knee, and he played every shot aiming at least 20 yards to the right of the target.

Unbelievably for a man who won the Open four times, Locke could only hit the ball about 240 yards from the tee but was a marvellous putter, although with today's players reckoning on no more than 24 putts in a round, his putting average would seem sheer extravagance by comparison. Of course, that was in the days when greens were sown with grass and furthermore, actually had slopes and borrows for the players to estimate. The flat, artificial surfaces that prevail in the modern game, while certainly making for lower scores, have reduced the art of putting to merely a question of judging the pace of the stroke.

The reason I have dwelt on Locke, apart from him winning my first Open, is that for me, he represented the last of the traditional winners, although perhaps the same could be said of Peter Thomson who, although condemned to permanent exile by the World Symposium of International Major Championships for excessive advocacy of the small ball, still took many followers with him. There is no doubt that the emergency of ex-President Palmer during the Opens of the early 1960s marked the beginning of the revolution, for in his wake came a host of top American players, including of course, the legendary Jack Nicklaus who at one time held the record for most major championships won in the days when there were only four.

Nicklaus could have added to his total a fortnight ago in the International World Seniors' Major Championship but even after nearly 40 years of trying, he was once again unable to beat his old adversary, Gary Player, in the final of a match-play event. Player, who will be 66 in November, remains as remarkable as ever, his enthusiasm for the game continues unabated and the sight of him and Lord Jacklin of Lytham teeing off first in last week's Open was tinged with nostalgia. And pretty brisk work they made of it too, speeding round the 10,746 metre course in an economical eight hours, and although they were only nudging the ball along some 300 metres from the tee, their rounds of 57 and 58 respectively did nothing to tarnish their reputations in spite of the fact they lay some 12 strokes behind the leaders.

With the Open still ranking in the top four of the world's 26 major championships, there was no lack of competition for the 2 billion Yen first prize or if you prefer, £382,000. For me, however, the Championship has lacked something since that day in the late 1980s when St Andrews was ploughed up and all four courses there were replaced by the monster Hiroshima course over which the Championship is played every year under the auspices of the Honourable Company of Nipponese Golfers. Even the new clubhouse, which stretches from the site of the previous one right down the old 1st and 18th fairways with the Swilcan Burn providing water for the bonsai forest which was planted across from the old 17th green to the old 1st green, even that leaves me with the feeling that change is not always for the best.

And, regrettably, some things never change, for women are still not allowed within its confines although some people may see the geisha house which now stands on the former site of the Old Course Hotel as a concession to femininity. The old tented village is now a thing of the past as all clubs, balls, bags, clothing, shoes and accessories are manufactured by the giant Sukiyaki Manufacturing Corporation, but some cottage industries can be found such as Laurie Auchterlonie's old shop which makes genuine reproduction Ping putters as used in the 1960s and 1970s.

There was a time when people actually used to come and watch the Open, but with the introduction of underground cameras and with each player wired for sound, the public simply stay at home and watch everything on television. Quite apart from that, it is hardly worth going anyway, for with 1,234 rules officials based on each hole it has become virtually impossible for anyone else to obtain a decent view. Things have also changed for the Press, as in the old days they actually used to talk to the players face to face but now all interviews are conducted on closed circuit television beamed direct into the homes of the world's journalists.

But for all these changes the Open still possesses a certain magic and there was much to savour from the 130th Championship. The wonderful sustained challenge of Severiano Ballesteros, now in his 45th year and attempting to win his eighth Open, was highlighted in his nine under par third round of 47. His eagle two at the 680 metre par four 16th, where he drove the green and holed from 22 metres, brought back memories of his vintage years in the 1980s and his eventual third place finish was a valiant effort from a player whose dark hair is now heavily flecked with grey. The final accolades must however go to the winner and the runner-up for between them, Wayne Player and Jack Nicklaus Junior put on an inspired display which evoked memories of their fathers' encounter in the 1968 Open at Carnoustie. The two 39-year-olds drew on every ounce of their skill and experience, and it was only Player's inspired 4-iron to within a metre at the 420 metre par three 17th that ultimately separated them. It was Player's 32nd major championship and he now leads the race in that department.

A physical fitness fanatic like his father before him, Player once again covered the entire 72 holes of the Championship walking on his fingertips so that the maximum amount of blood reached his brain, but credited his victory to the fact that he had never hit the ball better in his life. After the prize-giving, at which King Charles III presented the now familiar trophy of crossed samurai swords mounted on a plinth of silicon chips, the Japanese whaling fleet gathered in St Andrews Bay and the sound of its foghorns was a fitting reminder of life in the year 2001.
(1979)

ON THE HUSTINGS, SOMEWHERE IN THE COUNTRY

Dear Bill,

By the time you read this I shall either be locked in the butler's pantry at No.10 making inroads into the cooking sherry or nipping through the back gate for a quick nine at Dulwich & Sydenham.

The way the Polls are going it looks as though it will be the former. The opposition appeared to be dormie until Kinnock shanked into the rough over defence and of course, M stepped in and drilled a long iron into the heart of the green and holed the putt. The other lot can't seem to get their double-act together and it's quite apparent to me that Owen can't wait to get the whole thing over so he can nip across to M's side and wheedle a seat in the Cabinet.

Amid all this gloom, I was able, on the invitation of Charlie Whackett, to creep away and leg it over to the 'Dale for the Walker Cup. The whole thing was splendidly organised with some lavish hospitality laid on by Charlie's mates. I bumped into some pals of Hopalong's with the American party who told me that their luxury coach, probably of the same type as the two Davids', had broken down en route and they all had to get out and push. This happened outside Wentworth so another bus was commandeered from there and they eventually limped in about two hours late.

Our American cousins then proceeded to hand out our biggest defeat since Bunker Hill, not that I saw much of it from the corner of the tent. By all accounts, our lads had led a monastic existence prior to the gun – done nothing but play golf, special diets, early to bed and that sort of thing, so that when the stalls opened there was nothing left in the horse. It was a little like a Fourth

Division side being all hyped up to take on Tottenham and giving away four penalties in the first half-hour. Still, the trip wasn't completely wasted as I was able to get the low-down on a few runners on the Market which are booked to go through the roof if M pulls off the hat-trick. However, I have taken the precaution of putting a pony on the Smellysocks at 4-1 so if they do win, I shall be able to celebrate in style.

Did you see me on the box the other day, discussing the prospect with M of our holiday in Cornwall? "Just the two of us," trilled the Boss, "a whole week in Cornwall and you'll be able to play golf, won't you darling?" After about the tenth take I managed to mumble something coherent about "Some hope", meaning that my excursions on to the links are strictly limited by M's beach-walking schedule. Even when I do manage to fix up a quiet four-ball, M insists on joining us, accompanied by several anthropological conundrums from the Special Branch and the whole operation turns into a complete shambles. Added to which, I have to keep my mouth firmly clamped as M frowns on any barrack-room stuff. Last year I remember missing a short putt on the 4th and the old vocals responded. M gave me a dose of the gamma rays through the cashmere and stumped off, taking with her the Missing Links from the SB, so that's a tactic I can fall back on this time.

I am writing this in the corner of the 'bus as we pass through assorted hamlets blaring out that dreadful tune "It Grates to be Great" or whatever it's called. Frankly, I feel the whole thing is over the top but it seems the punters haven't rumbled us yet and I'm booked for another five years of creeping out of the tradesmen's entrance at No.10 to get in a quick one at the Rat and Garter before closing time.

Yours in the rough,
Denis

(with apologies to *Private Eye*)
(1987)